Interpretive
Planning

The **5-M Model**
for Successful
Planning Projects

interpPress

THE—
NATIONAL
ASSOCIATION FOR
INTERPRETATION

P.O. Box 2246
Fort Collins, CO 80522

NAI is a private nonprofit [501(c)3] organization and professional association. NAI's mission is: "Inspiring leadership and excellence to advance natural and cultural interpretation as a profession." For information, visit www.interpnet.com.

ISBN 1-879931-12-5

Printed in Singapore.

To Les
for his patience and support

and my exceptional boys
Travis and Trevor
for challenging me to do things that matter

CONTENTS

When I was a young state park interpreter and still knew everything (an idea that wore off long ago), I decided the park needed a trail for visually disabled people. A lot of trails for folks with various kinds of disabilities were being built in the early 1970s. I simply wrote a grant proposal that surprised me by being funded. I had not really approached this from any scientifically determined need, so the serendipitous goodness of an easy grant put a smile on my face. I quickly determined that the trail would have a smooth—perhaps concrete—surface, no steps (despite rugged terrain), a kickrail for those using a cane and Braille interpretive signs. I had seen the movie *The Miracle Worker* about Helen Keller and thought myself prepared to plan this trail.

The next piece of luck was even more simple. I had been teaching biology as a graduate assistant and one of my students from those days had become the county social services program manager for visually disabled people. She was legally blind and understood her audience well. When she happened to go through the visitor center I managed, we engaged in a conversation about the new trail, prompting her to make a very thoughtful offer. "Let's bring blind people from the community out here and let them experience the area first and give you ideas." I liked the idea. They came out and quickly explained that few blind people read Braille and many do not use a white cane. They thought a wood-chip trail with gravel bars indicating steps or direction changes would be more fun. "We're just like you. We come to a park to explore and have a sense of adventure. Concrete trails would be too much like the city for this setting. A cassette recorder would better suit their needs to hear interpretive stories," they explained. Their ideas cost less money, served their needs better, and created a trail popular with virtually all people because it was not overly specialized for a population that did not really exist.

I had never before heard of interpretive planning, and just plain luck saved this interpretive project from being a waste of money. The trail still exists and gets a lot of use by all people. I really needed a planning process to help me understand that crafting interpretive media for specific audiences can be done successfully. I did some things right—like having a kind of informal focus group with the intended audience—but I certainly had no plan. I tripped over a process due to the good advice of a former student. I would have loved a book on interpretive planning. I could have used thoughtful, experienced advice from a professional planner. Even then I would have appreciated that. Now that resource exists.

You have picked up a very valuable book if you are developing an interpretive plan or want to work as an interpretive planning consultant. It is also a valuable tool if you'll be working with a consultant or planner within your agency, as it contains ideas on how to select a consultant qualified to do the job you need. *Interpretive Planning: The 5-M Model for Successful Planning Projects* is quite simply the best possible resource currently available for guiding you on any interpretive planning project.

If you've ever worked with the author, Lisa Brochu, you'll know that she answers most planning questions she's asked with, "It depends." Is she avoiding answering tough questions? No, usually she is challenging the planning team to think—and not react—to complex situations with "cookie-cutter" solutions. She devoutly believes in the vital role planners can play when they understand this process and can thoughtfully apply it to a new situation. Interpretive planners must learn to ask the right questions and study the most appropriate resource materials to be effective in creating options and making decisions about an interpretive site or program.

Interpretive Planning: The 5-M Model for Successful Planning Projects is the culmination of Lisa's twenty-five years of creating interpretive plans. The book explains a process she has refined and taught to hundreds of planners and interpreters wanting to communicate effectively with their audiences through diverse media.

Why is such a model necessary? Tens of millions of dollars are wasted each year at parks, zoos, museums, visitor center, nature centers, aquariums and historic sites when ineffective facilities and exhibits are built. These projects often start with the hope that planning dollars can be saved by cutting quickly to the product. But when money is invested in a sign, exhibit, brochure or building without a careful planning process, goals and objectives are rarely accomplished. In the worst situations you will frustrate your guests and make them wonder what folly inspired your project.

The National Association for Interpretation (NAI) defines interpretation as "forging emotional and intellectual connections between the interests of the audience and the inherent meanings of the resource." The 5-M Model works from this basic definition in helping you, as a planner, understand the many variables that must be balanced in a well-planned interpretive project. The model values both the cognitive processes of doing thorough research with analysis while also honoring the importance of creativity. There are always many "right" ways to approach a project and a planner should facilitate an understanding of what options will best achieve the mission, goals, and objectives of the organization.

More and more organizations and agencies are interested in hiring planners and consultants who are well-trained and have relevant experience. This planning book stands alone or serves as a great companion to a planning course or seminar. You can read it and apply much of what is in it immediately. You can also find regular planning courses, often taught by Lisa, through NAI and get hands-on experience with planning using the 5-M Model. This course can also lead to you earning NAI's Certified Interpretive Planner (CIP) credential.

Interpretive planners learn from this model that they will never have all the answers, but they can become masters of asking the right questions to create the most appropriate options. If you employ this very practical and effective planning model, Lisa will soon have you answering questions by saying, "It depends."

—Tim Merriman, Ph.D.
Executive Director
National Association for Interpretation

PREFACE

When it comes to interpretive planning, it seems no matter what the question is, the answer is almost always, "It depends." After working on literally hundreds of projects and coaching dozens of budding interpretive planners, I have come to believe that "It depends" is the single most valuable lesson to be learned about planning an interpretation project. Since I have seldom found that flexibility expressed in existing literature about interpretive planning, I thought the time had come to put whatever wisdom I have gained through more than twenty-five years of fieldwork into print. Originally, I thought it would be nice to write the definitive textbook on interpretive planning, but after having spent the last several years helping new planners get on their feet, I thought a better approach might be simply to write the things that I tell them. So what you have here is not the last word on what interpretive planning is or should be—instead, it's the running narrative that you might get if you followed me around to visitor centers, museums, nature centers, state parks, botanical gardens, or any other interpretive venue.

Right up front, I'd like to acknowledge four individuals who have contributed vastly to my approach to interpretive planning. Each influenced me in different ways, but all contributed to my professional development and have had some influence over the practices I employ in interpretive planning. My sincere thanks go to Tom Christensen, John Hanna, Corky McReynolds and Tim Merriman for their contributions to the interpretive field and to my own personal and professional growth along the way.

I would also like to thank those people who took the time to read the manuscript and provide thoughtful comments prior to publication. Any errors are certainly mine and not theirs. Specifically, I'd like to thank Douglas Knudson for his editorial assistance. Though we don't always agree, I have a great deal of respect for his opinion and appreciate the time he took to help me improve the manuscript. I would also like to thank Tim Merriman for his generous donation of numerous photographs that appear throughout the book.

Throughout the book, I have tried to credit anyone whose work I have consulted or adapted over the years. If I've missed a credit, please bring it to my attention for the second edition. Some ideas have been around such a long time and have been adapted so many times, they can be difficult to attribute properly, especially if they were the result of convergent evolution of thought rather than specifically borrowed from others. Certainly, no omission was intentional.

The photographs in the book were taken at a variety of locations. I have attempted to show good examples rather than negative examples (though I admit they were harder to find). It should be noted that few of the photos shown reflect my own planning work. I seek out good examples wherever they occur and of course, I am somewhat limited in the number of examples I can show. In almost every case, when I asked the site staff about the planner and designer of the building, landscape, or exhibit features pictured in these photographs, the response was simply a blank look.

The purpose of this book is to help you understand that interpretive planning is a process, not a product. This book is not filled with scientific research and rhetoric, and so I offer my humble apologies to the academic community right up front. I believe that research is a valuable component of the interpretive field, helping us to understand why some things work and others don't. I heartily encourage testing of ideas throughout the process of planning and sharing the results of those tests with the greater interpretive community. But I'm not a researcher or academician, so that is not the approach you'll find here. Instead, I've tried to document what works in the field, based on more than twenty-five years of experience with a variety of projects. Many of the ideas incorporated here are general rules of thumb that seem to work well, rather than scientifically based theories.

In addition to providing consultant services for almost three decades, I've been a visitor center manager and a field interpreter. I've created nonprofit organizations and been employed by a state agency. I know what works, though I can't always pin down the theoretical underpinnings that would support my conviction. Because of the variety of projects in which I've been involved, I've always thought that it would be impossible to offer a cookbook solution with step-by-step instructions for interpretive planning. Good planning just doesn't work that way. Again, I offer apologies to those who feel compelled to follow checklists and fill out forms. You won't find them here.

Indeed, you should document the process you choose to follow in a product called an interpretive plan, and matrices and forms may help some people do that. I am becoming increasingly fond of tables that help organize information when it seems appropriate. But to remember that the most important part of the plan document is the process that you use to create it, not the pretty paper in which it's wrapped. The true end product is not that document, it is the success of your visitors' experiences that ultimately results in the overall success of your site and organization.

This book recognizes that interpretation is both an art and a science, which has long been established by professors and practitioners in this field. Doesn't it stand to reason that planning for interpretation must also have elements of both art and science? And because interpretive planning combines art (intuition and creativity) and science (research and response to cold, hard facts), there is simply no one right way to do it. This book features a planning model that provides a framework, but not a template. It is designed to help you develop a process that allows you to be successful in meeting management objectives by creating the most effective interpretation for a given situation.

I hope that you will take the information presented here and adapt it to your specific needs and planning style as you get started as an interpretive planner or work with professional planners you may hire. This book will not make you an expert overnight. After more than a quarter-century of experience, I still don't have all the answers. Because each site is unique, I constantly come across situations that challenge me to find innovative and creative, yet realistic solutions. But once I recognized that a single process doesn't work in every situation, I was able to develop a flexible framework that can be applied to almost any planning project to get results that are most appropriate for that project.

I have deliberately avoided giving details regarding the planning and design of specific media in this book. There are several excellent references available that focus on planning and design of signs, exhibits, and other interpretive media. Instead, this book is intended to give you the bigger picture and help you determine what media might best communicate the message, given the parameters of your site's resources. It is about interpretive planning, not design.

Finally, I hope that you understand that the purchase of this book and even careful study of its pages will not create easy solutions for the challenges you may face as an interpretive planner. It's not the book (or the plan) that takes action, it's people like you that apply their new-found knowledge that make the difference. This book is a tool—how you use what you learn from it will determine the extent of positive change you're able to accomplish.

—Lisa Brochu
Certified Interpretive Planner

You're on a family vacation traveling through western Colorado. Though it hasn't exactly been like a day at the office, tension is beginning to run a little high. With you, your spouse, two young children, your mother-in-law, and the family dog encased in a single mini-van, you look for every opportunity to stop the vehicle, take a breather, and distract yourself and the others by learning a little about the country through which you're traveling. This particular morning, you've driven for several hours without encountering any likely prospects for such a stop. Then a sign along the highway indicates an interpretive stop ahead.

This is perfect, you think. You recognize the binocular logo on the sign, and, knowing that your family loves watching wildlife, you pull into the parking lot with high expectations. But when the kids pile out of the car, there are no interpretive or directional signs to guide your experience. Worse yet, there are no restroom facilities, no drinking water, and no place where the dog and children can stretch their legs safely. About fifty yards away, you spy a kiosk with what appears to be a few faded posters pocked with bullet holes, but you can't locate any sort of trailhead that would give you access to the kiosk without trampling through a very soggy wetland. Disappointed, you gather the troops, pile into the vehicle, and head back onto the highway, thinking uncharitable thoughts about whatever agency pulled this joke on unsuspecting tourists. My tax dollars at work, you sigh.

After an hour's travel, you see another brown highway sign denoting an interpretive stop. Though wary after your last experience, you agree with the family that it's time for a break. So once again, you pull off, but with lowered expectations. This time, however, attractive signs clearly mark the parking area, the restroom facility complete with drinking fountain and pay phone, the dog-walking area, and the trailhead. Everyone, even the dog, takes the opportunity to attend to their basic needs. Refreshed, you return Fido to the car, leaving him stretched out comfortably with a bowl of water in the shade. You approach the trailhead and find a colorful and informative sign that shows the trail route, approximate walking time, and what you might expect to find along the way.

Your interest is piqued and your schedule will allow time for this pleasant diversion, so off you go down the universally accessible trail. Within a minute, you come to a sign. Brightly colored artwork immediately grabs your attention. You read the fifty words of text aloud to your family. They chuckle over the sign's lighthearted approach to interpreting the fishing behavior of great blue herons, when suddenly, your youngest child points out a heron on the far side of the pond. Immediately, your spouse (showing off new-found knowledge) paraphrases the sign text in a quiet voice while the bird continues fishing undisturbed. Feeling like they now know this heron on a personal basis, your family watches for a while and jointly comes to some additional conclusions about the bird's natural history based on their observations and the tidbits of information gleaned from the interpretive sign. After the entire walk is done and you're returning to your vehicle, your mother-in-law spontaneously picks up a discarded six-pack plastic ring, having been made aware through interpretive signage that such items can be fatal to wading birds.

These are two very real scenarios. Which was the more successful, in terms of addressing visitor expectations, altering visitor behavior, creating visitor satisfaction, and achieving management objectives? What made the difference between the two situations? If you answered good planning, you're on the right track. Certainly, the design and placement of engaging features in the second locale had a hand in the greater success of this experience. But someone first had to decide what they hoped to accomplish, whom it was for, what the message was to be, how to design and deliver that message, and where to locate it. That is what planning is all about. In the first scenario, without conscious application of logic to these many decisions, time and dollars were inevitably wasted and worst of all, the people theoretically served by the agency were alienated. In the second stop, a judicious planning process helped the clientele become informed allies, each coming away from the experience with a gratifying sense of internal satisfaction.

A Definition of Interpretive Planning
If you've picked up this book, you probably already have an idea of what interpretation is. The National Association for Interpretation defines it as "a communication process that forges intellectual and emotional connections

between the interests of the visitor and the meanings inherent in the resource." This definition is important to remember no matter what your planning project may be. Too often, the idea of making connections gets lost in the zeal to demonstrate just how much information one visitor center can hold. The one thing missing from the NAI definition is an acknowledgement that interpretation serves a purpose. It should help accomplish the mission of the site and management objectives or there's little reason to spend money on it. Although the altruistic nature of most interpretive efforts is laudable, the real reason for providing interpretive services is to build support for the agency and to encourage a sense of stewardship for the resource. In other words, interpretation should go beyond making connections to the next logical step of making a difference.

Interpretive planning, then, is the decision-making process that blends management needs and resource considerations with visitor desire and ability to pay (with time, interest, and/or dollars) to determine the most effective way to communicate the message to targeted markets. Planning for interpretation allows us to deliver messages through the creation of experiences. Some of these experiences may include interaction with interpretive media, while others may be carefully constructed to seem serendipitous, allowing self-discovery of the resource at hand. Walking around a bend in a trail to behold a first glimpse of the Grand Canyon is not necessarily enhanced by an interpretive wayside exhibit but the experienced planner will know that careful placement of the trail can allow the experience to occur.

Too often, the interpretive planning process is short-circuited in the mistaken belief that one size fits all or that one media type can effectively communicate any message to anyone in any setting. Failure to consider the many variables surrounding an interpretive opportunity leads to an interpretive monoculture where the tendency is to fall back on basics and simply prescribe what is most familiar. A state parks director once exhorted all of his park managers to "go out there and build a self-guided trail in every one of your parks." In the rush to provide a physical product, the effectiveness of that product was unquestioned until someone noticed that in some parks there really wasn't a good place for a trail; in others, the trail ended up being too hard to maintain; and in still others, the visitors had other interests and never used the constructed trail. In the meantime, several tens of thousands of dollars and man-hours were wasted on trail construction and maintenance.

Effective interpretive planning, thoughtfully approached and addressing a wide array of variables, should always lead to success because it is a marriage of **management, message, market, mechanics,** and **media.** These are

LISA BROCHU

Participants in the Certified Interpretive Planner class offered by the National Association for Interpretation work in small groups to complete a planning project at the host site. Each group presents its findings and recommendations at the end of the five-day course.

the five Ms that form a planning framework whether your project involves a single exhibit or a statewide effort. This book examines each of the five Ms separately in later chapters, but a brief description of each would include:

Management The "nuts and bolts" associated with running the interpretive operation. Includes mission, goals, policies, issues, and operational resources such as budget, staffing, and maintenance.

Message The ideas that will be communicated to the visiting public. Includes theme, subtheme, and storylines based on resource, audience, and management and considerations.

Market The users and supporters, both current and those who might have an interest in the subject or site in the future; and the implications of targeted market segments, and market position.

Mechanics The large- and small-scale physical properties that have some effect or influence on what is being planned.

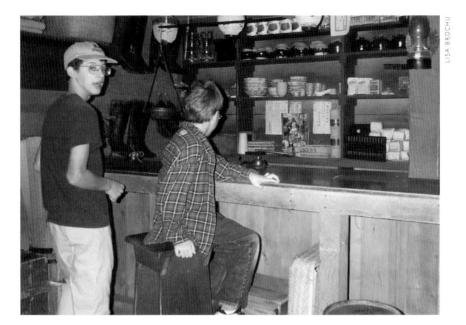

Dioramas at the High Desert Museum create an immersion experience with sights, sounds, smells, temperature, and fans. In this Chinese apothecary, an audio recording of the owners moving around in the back room brings the historical diorama to life.

Media The most effective method(s), given the mechanics of the situation, for communicating messages to targeted market segments in support of management objectives.

The 5-M Model is not rocket science. It's not even really anything new or unusual. In fact, it's simply a common sense way to remember all the considerations that should affect the decision-making process. Ignoring any of these pieces leaves the planner with an incomplete puzzle, leading to ineffective interpretation. Taking each of these five elements into account to answer the question "Upon what does it depend?" directs your planning process to creative and diverse solutions.

Types of Planning Projects

One of the challenges commonly faced by planners is the lack of consistent terminology within the profession of interpretation. One park's comprehensive plan may be a nature center's interpretive prospectus, or vice versa. Planning consultants often develop their own lexicon or simply go along with whatever their client wants to call the document, adding to the confusion about what should be included in a "plan." For the purposes of this book, the following terms will be used as defined below.

Master Plan or Comprehensive Plan

This type of plan represents substantial effort from a multidisciplinary team. Ideally, the master plan (sometimes called a comprehensive plan or comprehensive master plan) looks at the entire operation, not just interpretation. Facilities, site development, landscape features, operations, programming, and interpretive media will be blended into a holistic plan that provides guidance for operations and development within a projected planning horizon (usually somewhere between three and eight years, with the most common being five). The master plan is critical for a new site; however, it should be a process that is revisited and updated every five to ten years for sites already in operation to ensure that changing market characteristics, site characteristics, and technology are not ignored.

At a bare minimum, the planning team will generally include specialists in architecture, landscape architecture, interpretive planning (which includes market analysis), and management. Specialists in engineering, exhibit design, and education may also be needed, but often, they can be brought in later as specific components of the plan are fleshed out. The master plan, though it contains extensive and valuable overall direction, will often paint broad brush strokes with guidance for completing individual component plans as necessary. If contracted, expect this type of plan to run anywhere from $10,000 to $100,000 or more, depending on the specifications of the project (size, location, issues, level of detail required, etc.). It may take anywhere from three months to a year to complete depending on the complexities of the site.

Interpretation Plan or Interpretation & Education Plan

This plan focuses on the interpretive or education (or combination thereof) component of an operation. While a good interpretive plan will certainly take architectural, site, and operational issues into consideration, these elements are included to provide background and parameters to the discussion of specific interpretive media (both personal and nonpersonal). An interpretation plan—or I&E—plan will provide details about the overall interpretive or education program, thematic guidelines, cost projections for development and implementation, and media descriptions that match selected media to audiences and objectives.

The interpretive plan is usually completed by an interpretive planner who has some background in market analysis, management skills, and interpretation fundamentals, as well as experience working with architects, landscape architects, interpreters, exhibit/sign designers, and fabricators. This type of plan may sometimes require site-planning expertise. Depending on the level of expertise required, some planners may elect to bring in a landscape architect to render a site plan, while others will be comfortable performing this function on their own if a registered landscape architect's plan is not required to avoid liability issues. For instance, if the plan is conceptual in nature, it may involve placing theoretical bubbles or lines on a base map to represent potential general locations of interpretive features. If this is the case, then the planner can certainly complete that task. However, if it's necessary to create a base map, or provide elevations showing construction notes for trails, decks, or other constructed features, or the plan must take into consideration drainages, buried lines, or other landscape technicalities beyond the experience of the planner, then the services of a registered landscape architect are definitely called for. If contracted, expect to pay between $5,000 and $50,000 and take three to six months to prepare an interpretation plan, depending on the specifications of the project.

Interpretive Prospectus

If you check the dictionary, you will see that "plan" is defined as a document or drawing that provides details about how to accomplish something, while "prospectus" is defined as a summary of a particular venture. These terms are often used interchangeably in the interpretive world, but perhaps they shouldn't be. Technically speaking, a prospectus is designed to provide only enough detail to interest a potential funder. In other words, it may be either an executive summary of an interpretive plan or a summary of a proposed planning process (with suggested outcomes) used to secure funding for that process, but it is not the plan itself. Having said that, there are agencies and individuals that will continue to use the term prospectus to include a full-blown plan, and that's okay. But for the purposes of this book, a prospectus is a summary document designed to create support for the project at hand. As defined here, a prospectus may cost between $2,500 and $10,000 and require about one to three months to complete, depending on the complexity of the project and the quality of the products desired. It is usually created by either an interpretive planner working alone or in conjunction with a marketing specialist. Because it is used to create support, the final product may also need the touch of a graphic designer to make it visually appealing to its intended audience.

Information or interpretation? Information and orientation signs help guide visitors to potential interpretive opportunities, so they need to be considered in the planning effort.

Interpretive Exhibit Plan or Program Plan

This plan further focuses the efforts of the interpretive plan described above. While the interpretive plan (or I&E plan) takes an overall view of the interpretive program at a site, a specific media plan will concentrate on a targeted area. The most common areas targeted for planning are exhibits or programs, although many sites will simply separate personal and nonpersonal media, incorporating publications, signs, and other nonpersonal media into an exhibit plan. This plan is what many sites will request when they need to update an exhibit gallery or rethink their program structure to address changing markets. It lets them know what their options are and how much it will cost to accomplish their objectives. Occasionally, a media plan will uncover the need to rethink the entire operation, leading to a full-blown master planning effort. More frequently, this type of plan provides the focus needed to address a single key issue in a cost-effective way. The media plan is usually completed by an interpretive planner with experience in working with publications, exhibit design and fabrication, or interpretive programs. If concept sketches of nonpersonal media are requested, a graphic artist or illustrator may also be needed. If contracted, it may cost anywhere from $2,500 to $25,000 and take from one to six months, depending on the complexity of the project.

Sign Plan

Although it's true that signs can be considered nonpersonal media and therefore may be incorporated into a media plan such as that previously described, a typical sign plan is quite different from a media plan. A sign plan features an inventory of each and every sign at a site, including directional, information, and interpretive signs. Directional signs are those that provide names of streets and specific locations, or that point visitors towards parking, trails, entries, exits, and other key features. Information signs are the ones that post rules and regulations, hours of operation, emergency contacts, and other items necessary for the safety or comfort of visitors. Interpretive signs contain a thematic message and often feature attractive illustrations, three-dimensional components (which constitutes a wayside exhibit), and engaging text.

The sign plan provides a comprehensive look at how people move through the site, often encouraging a more streamlined approach to signing. The location of each sign will be indicated on a site map. The plan will also include design guidelines to ensure consistency within and between the different categories of signs, as well as maintenance and replacement information. Concept sketches of sign layout, with text and suggested graphics are usually included. The sign plan may be undertaken by an interpretive planner working alone or with a landscape architect. Many sign plans are now prepared on databases or using Geographic Information Systems (GIS) mapping technology. Depending on the size and complexity of the site, and the level of detail desired, the sign plan may range from $5,000 to $50,000 and take anywhere from three months to a year to complete.

Strategic Plan

The strategic plan helps define a vision and mission for an organization. It also establishes or clarifies goals, objectives, and strategies for accomplishing specific tasks within a fairly short-term horizon. (See Chapter 5 for definitions of vision, mission, goals, objectives, and strategies.) The strategic plan can be a good starting point for a new site to help focus a steering committee or board's direction. It can also be a good planning tool for an existing site or organization to assess whether the original mission is still valid or to kick-start management overcome by inertia. Because strategic plans are short-term by nature, many organizations will elect to complete a strategic planning process on a regular basis, updating their strategic plan every two to three years. The only danger in this approach is that it may help the organization avoid identifying and planning for long-term needs. A more productive process is to use a strategic plan to get going and then follow up with long-range or annual business planning needs identified by the strategic-planning process.

Most strategic plans can be developed in a group process facilitated by an experienced planner over two to three days for a cost of $2,500 to $5000. The importance of using an outside facilitator to guide a strategic planning process cannot be stressed strongly enough. Though most types of planning can be done in-house if qualified staff are available, the nature of strategic planning usually requires an objective third party to allow thoughtful expression from all participants in an open atmosphere. A skilled facilitator can move the group beyond any sticking points and should end a productive session with a document that summarizes and filters the group discussion.

Long-Range Plan

The contents of a long-range plan will vary according to the type of agency or organization for which it is developed, but generally speaking, it involves looking at a ten-year planning horizon. It may include some of the elements of a comprehensive plan or it may be the classic "big picture" plan that gives the agency or organization a blueprint for achieving its vision. It is a good complement to a series of strategic-planning sessions. The long-range plan provides a framework for selectively planning specific short-term projects through each strategic planning process that takes place during the lifetime of the long-range plan. If contracted, a long-range plan may cost from $10,000 to $25,000 and take three to six months to complete.

Business Plan

The business plan is a critical document in the operation of an interpretive site (or any other business venture). The business plan, updated annually, summarizes factors from the previous and upcoming years that will influence business decisions for the next fiscal year. The best business plans are usually less than a dozen pages long. The plan should include specific strategies that will help accomplish previously determined long-range goals and objectives, including any budget or staff implications that might affect the accomplishment of those objectives.

Business plans are generally written by the executive director, superintendent, or whoever is responsible for managing the annual budget. In government agencies, where the budget is handed down from above, a business plan will still help determine the most effective ways to manage the money and account for its expenditure at year's end.

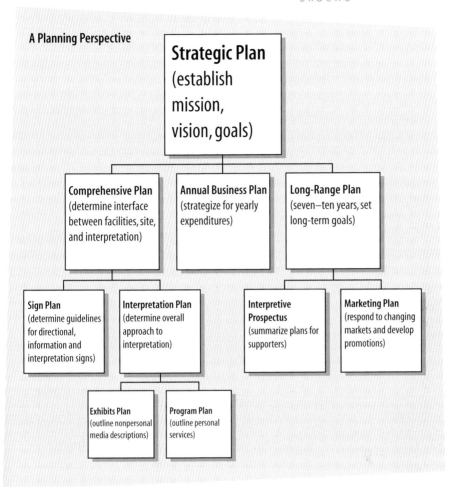

A Planning Perspective

Strategic Plan (establish mission, vision, goals)

Comprehensive Plan (determine interface between facilities, site, and interpretation)

Annual Business Plan (strategize for yearly expenditures)

Long-Range Plan (seven–ten years, set long-term goals)

Sign Plan (determine guidelines for directional, information and interpretation signs)

Interpretation Plan (determine overall approach to interpretation)

Interpretive Prospectus (summarize plans for supporters)

Marketing Plan (respond to changing markets and develop promotions)

Exhibits Plan (outline nonpersonal media descriptions)

Program Plan (outline personal services)

Marketing Plan

The marketing plan serves two functions. It provides an analysis of the current market climate surrounding a site or organization, and it provides recommendations for responding to that market climate through promotions and product strategies. The marketing plan can stand separately, but can also be integrated into an interpretive plan or master plan. Certainly, market analysis should be part of any planning effort, but the marketing plan, when standing alone, may go more in-depth into advertising and promotions or creation of a brand identity, logo, or slogan.

Interpretive planners with experience in market analysis can prepare a marketing plan; however, many agencies prefer to hire market-research companies or university professors to conduct research and analysis and then have advertising firms create a promotions plan and brand identity. It is important that an interpretive planner be included on the team if market-research or advertising firms are hired, to ensure that an appropriate thematic approach is considered. Additionally, the audience for interpretive sites is somewhat specialized and requires an understanding of visitor behavior that may be lacking in some research and advertising firms. Including an interpretive planner on the team can bring the visitor viewpoint to the table. If contracted, a marketing plan may range from $5,000 to $50,000, depending on the level of research and product development required, and usually takes three months to a year to complete.

Putting Plans into Perspective

Recognizing the need for a plan is an important first step in accomplishing any project. Determining which type of plan will best suit the need is the next step. Just as there is no one right way to approach a planning process, there is no single solution to the "Which plan should we do first?" dilemma. Where to start depends on what's already been done, who needs results and when, and what the ultimate goal of the planning process is.

The diagram on page 11 is not meant to suggest that there is necessarily a logical flow to planning any of these pieces, but is provided to illustrate potential relationships between various types of plans.

Generally speaking, it makes sense to plan from larger scale to smaller. Completing a strategic plan that outlines the mission, vision, and broad goals of the organization should probably come before detailing the exhibits and programs that will follow. Similarly, completing a comprehensive plan will provide big-picture guidance for individual interpretive components. But some of these plans can, and often should, easily become intertwined— for instance, strategic planning may, in some instances, be a part of the comprehensive or long-range planning process. A marketing plan or interpretive prospectus may be needed in conjunction with an exhibit plan. Whatever components make sense for a given situation are the ones that should be used.

To avoid stagnation, a thoughtful organization will almost always be in a planning phase of some sort. However, it is also possible to engage in planning activities to the extent that no plans can actually ever be carried out. Consider the workplace an ocean of activity. Each work station is a little tidepool, sometimes placid and sometimes swirling with new ideas. In the perfect system, there will be regular ebb and flow of planning cycles that keep the whole workplace healthy, yet still allow completion of the projects being planned.

An Abbreviated History of Interpretive Planning

The evolution of planning for interpretation has paralleled interpretive program planning, increasing in complexity as interpretive programming has grown in its scope. Early interpreters such as Enos Mills and John Muir often limited their program planning to studying the areas in which they led people or attempting to gain support for preservation of these areas. But even in these limited plans, there was a conscious development of how the message or area was to be presented to enlist support for its preservation. These and other crusaders were on a mission to affect behavior leading to preservation of what are now considered some of our prime interpretive resources.

Throughout the first half of the twentieth century, many different types of interpretive media became popular with visitors to historic sites and natural areas. Evening talks, guided walks, and interpretive signs were in wide use by the 1950s. Some master plans had begun to incorporate provisions for enhancing the visitor's experience through what was to later become accepted as "interpretation."

The end of World War II and a myriad of sociological factors put millions of travelers in cars searching out the world's natural and cultural hot spots. Many of these travelers expressed a curiosity often satisfied by historical plaques and point of interest markers—most of which were erected without any thought given to planning and ended up being more informative in nature than interpretive. But General Eustus P. Heredity's family wanted to see that he was remembered, and so interpretive media took on a look still familiar today in many places displaying history on a stick.

Mission 66 reflected one of the first—if not the first—large-scale, agency-wide attempts at interpretive planning. Interpretive planning arrived on a grand scale in a ten-year program aimed at upgrading National Park Service physical facilities, including interpretation. Most of the national parks and monuments were subjected to a standard interpretive treatment including a visitor center with an information desk, exhibits, and an audiovisual program often beginning with the phrase, "Millions of years ago, this area was covered with a vast inland sea." In spite of this often uniform treatment, the value of interpretive planning became apparent as a ten-year transformation of interpretation in the national parks took place. A necessary outgrowth of the Mission 66 interpretive-planning effort was the development of a designated center for national parks to develop and implement media that had been planned. The Harpers Ferry Design Center entered the scene and became known as an industry standard synonymous with excellence in design. With increasing sophistication, interpretive planning became more specialized with interpretive concept plans, master plans, and design development standards for specific media.

Interpretive planning was not just evolving at the government level. Throughout the 1960s and '70s, historic sites and their related associations were realizing the economic value of well-planned interpretation. Nature centers and environmental education facilities began planning for interpretation well in advance of Earth Day. Bryan Ashbaugh headed up a nature center planning service for The Audubon Society that included a heavy dose of interpretive planning. In many of the major metropolitan areas, interpretive planning paralleled—though was rarely integrated with—park planning in city and county systems.

Associations such as the Society for the Interpretation of British Heritage, Interpretation Canada, the Association of Interpretive Naturalists (AIN), and the Western Interpreters Association (WIA) were growing rapidly and including many in their ranks who considered themselves interpretive planners. Articles on interpretive planning began to appear in their journals. Professional meetings of these and other associations included presentations on planning. By the mid-1970s, some university interpretive curricula included interpretive planning at undergraduate and graduate levels.

Over the next twenty years, several books were written about interpretation, but few touched on interpretive master planning in a meaningful way, instead focusing on product or program development. Yet the need for thoughtful planning became more critical as operational resources became more scarce and our nation's natural and cultural resources became more threatened. Most federal agencies responsible for interpretive sites, including the Bureau of Land Management, U.S. Fish and Wildlife Service, USDA Forest Service, and U.S. Army Corps of Engineers began to implement agency-oriented planning approaches and include material on interpretive planning in their agency training events.

In 1998, the National Association for Interpretation (which came about as the result of the consolidation of AIN and WIA in 1988) implemented a certification program that included the category "Certified Interpretive Planner." Interpretive planning workshops had become a regular feature of the National Interpreters Workshop and the Interpretive Management Institute, sponsored by NAI. The first Certified Interpretive Planner class took place in Austin, Texas, in 2001, creating a new standard for the interpretive planning process.

The development of interpretive planning as a specialty has evolved over the last fifty years often with vastly different approaches offered by different agencies and authors. This brief review of planning history only

serves to point toward a future in which interpretive planning will continue
to evolve in exciting new directions.

Interpretive Planning Approaches

Interpretive planning is a process that involves both sides of the brain. While
there is some logical (left-brain) analysis that must be conducted, it is also a
creative (right-brain) process, usually limited only by budget and imagination.
This dichotomy means that there is no one, single, correct way to approach
interpretive planning. Most planners develop a process over time that is
comfortable for them and the people with whom they are planning. Good
planners understand that their process may need massaging to adapt to a
specific planning situation. In other words, the strongest planning approach
will be the one that is most appropriate for a particular project. The
common-sense consideration of the five Ms of management, message,
market, mechanics, and media should always be present, but the creative
analysis and treatment of the variables encountered is what will give the
plan its individual flavor.

Each planning approach has its own strengths and weaknesses, but all
sound planning approaches share these things in common (the five Ms):

Management An understanding of management requirements, needs, and
capabilities.

Markets An understanding of current and prospective customers and
market position

Message A strong and appropriate story about the available resources.

Mechanics An understanding of the physical opportunities and constraints
of the location.

Media An appropriate mix of methodologies to deliver the message(s) to the
market(s) within the constraints of management.

Planning approaches differ in the weight given to each of these five
components or by what drives the process.

Market-Based Planning

Usually one of the most successful methods of planning, the market-based
approach is driven to a large extent by the customer. Traditionally, interpretive
sites not run by commercial ventures fail to recognize their visitors as
customers, but that is, in fact, exactly what they are. Whether they pay entry
fees, parking fees, or simply tax dollars, visitors who choose to spend their
leisure time at an interpretive site are paying customers who increasingly

LISA BROCHU

The Great White Mystery at Newport, Oregon's Aquarium invites visitors to investigate what happened to Surfer Bob through an interactive exhibit experience capped off by a walk through a shark tunnel where visitors can see the suspects swim by. This creative exhibit plays on the common misconception that sharks are the "bad guys."

demand satisfaction. Sometimes management feels the need to deliver a message in which the customers are not necessarily interested. With thoughtful planning and an awareness of customer desires, management can couch their message in such a way that the customer base can respond appropriately and with enthusiasm. The market-based approach investigates customer needs and desires and creatively strives for customer satisfaction within the constraints imposed by management or a sensitive resource. So, for example, in a market-based approach to planning, we might recognize that visitors to the Badaling Gate of the Great Wall of China are coming to the area to visit the Great Wall. In an adjacent park, if management wants to deliver a message about environmental issues, they would do well to trade on the public's interest in the Great Wall. Instead of simply ignoring the Wall and talking about hawks that might be seen within the park, the media could take the viewpoint of the hawk looking down at the Great Wall or could describe how the Great Wall impacted the environmental conditions of what is now the park area, creating a link between the Wall and the habitat that can be seen today.

Visitors have the opportunity to learn more about shark facts and myths as they work their way through a series of "crime labs." As the experience comes to a close, visitors discover that Surfer Bob is fine, since sharks rarely attack people. Indirect visitor observation throughout this exhibit revealed a high percentage of interest, family interaction, and sharing of information.

Strengths Because the results directly relate to customer desires and ability to pay, this approach is usually relatively successful. When customers are satisfied, management also gets what it wants in the form of higher revenues, lowered maintenance, constituency support, resource protection, or similar objectives.

Weaknesses The approach requires a thorough understanding of a site's current and potential markets for effectiveness. Arriving at that understanding can be a time-consuming and costly process. Management often has little understanding of the concept of marketing or few available resources to pursue appropriate implementation actions.

Resource-Based Planning

The most frequently used method of planning, the resource-based approach focuses on the available resources, regardless of visitor interest. This approach is popular with agencies charged with protecting significant cultural or natural features. It's a twist on the "if you build it, they will come" philosophy, instead stating that "if it's there, they will come." It's true enough, to some extent. Clearly, a spectacular resource such as the Washington Monument or the Painted Desert will draw visitors, regardless of what other opportunities are offered. But interpretation is about more than just numbers of visitors or the provision of informative facts about a particular resource. Good interpretation also makes a difference in visitor behavior and understanding, provoking further thought and action.

Strengths This approach focuses messages on the obvious, so in some respects may be the easiest approach to use since the messages are predetermined. Thoughtful resource-based planning can actually help managers channel visitor movement and assist in protection of the resource.

Weaknesses Visitor motivations and interests are often overlooked, so cost-effectiveness of products (number of successful contacts) is usually low. It can be difficult to establish relevancy to customer's home environment.

Budget-Based Planning

Frequently mandated by available financial resources (or the lack thereof), the budget-based approach is quite simply a matter of what can be afforded. Given X amount of dollars, management goes shopping for whatever product(s) can be had for that amount, then writes the plan to justify those expenditures. The frightening reality of this approach is that it often impedes thinking about partnership possibilities, fund-raising, and use of volunteer programs to extend the potential for contributions towards more effective interpretation.

Strengths This approach is based in cold, hard reality. With only so many dollars available, there is only so much that can be done. It can sometimes force creative problem-solving.

Weaknesses Although a good planner can often work with an available budget to devise appropriate solutions to interpretive challenges, the budget-driven plan usually reflects little consideration of visitor desires, resource characteristics, or management objectives, and so the effectiveness of its products is potentially quite low.

Objective-Based Planning

The objective-based plan defines specific, measurable objectives for the plan and its products. It begins with the question, "What do we want to accomplish?" or, "How do we want to change visitor attitudes or behavior?" and then suggests methods for achieving the stated objectives. One of the real beauties of this type of planning process is that it identifies desired end results and, as the process and products are put into place, they can constantly be evaluated against the objectives.

Strengths The objective-based plan is one of the easiest to evaluate, because it provides a checklist for success. If objectives are realistic and grounded in a thorough assessment and analysis of key issues, audience, and management requirements, this approach can be highly successful.

Weaknesses This approach focuses on problem-solving, but inexperienced planners sometimes forget to define the problem before attempting to solve it. Expertise in writing objectives is required. Objective-based plans are often not revisited or evaluated.

Agency-Oriented Planning

Many agencies develop a template for interpretive planning to achieve some level of uniformity among their many units. Templates may include specific outlines, forms, or other "cookbook" methods for developing interpretive concepts. The agency develops a certain interpretive planning style or product that is expected to be carried through each site, regardless of individual site characteristics. These agency-oriented approaches were somewhat commonplace as interpretive planning was coming into vogue. As a result, interpretation certainly was broadly implemented but with a limited scope and marginal impact. More recently, agency-oriented approaches have encouraged varied inputs rather than giving the prescription for interpretation. In 1998, the Western Regional Office of the National Park Service introduced the Comprehensive Interpretive Planning Process for use with NPS site interpretive planning. While some uniformity might result, the intent is that the widest variety of inputs to the planning process will be considered.

Strengths Providing a template or agency style can be helpful for inexperienced planners to initiate the process. Developed products may help promote a sense of agency identity.

Weaknesses Templates and strict agency styles and products show little regard for the specific needs of individual situations. They may put boundaries on creative thinking and usually exhibit limited success.

Operations Planning

Operations planning has been used by some organizations, facilities, and agencies to fill in the gap between having an interpretive plan and no planning at all. Usually, the interpretive operations plan is a description of the actions that will be taken in support of interpretation for the current year. It often outlines the program schedule and may also call for the development of media or at least steps toward completing major projects. Operations planning is a wonderful process when used to implement an interpretive master plan. When it stands alone, it often reflects the interests of the interpreter of the moment and has a limited relationship to management, message, market, or media considerations. Operations planning often correlates to a strategic planning process, but is usually not subject to the same type of process, instead occurring in the vacuum of one interpreter's or manager's office.

Strengths Operations planning is an essential tool to carry out the action plan of the interpretive plan or master plan. It is based on the realities of current staffing and budget, allowing identification of short-term or annual actions that will take place.

Weaknesses It may lack a strong relationship to management, message, market, and media if there is no interpretive plan to back up the operations plan.

Summary

No matter which type of plan you need to complete, recognize that there are a number of approaches that may be appropriate. Which one is right for a particular project will depend on a number of factors unique to that project. Within the market-based approach, many planners approach visitor observation very systematically to better understand their customers. The resource-based approach is often used to answer the question, "What is so important about this place that we will allocate resources to tell that story to the customers?" Budget-based planning can lead planners through exercises to determine the cost effectiveness and efficiency of different media approaches. Agency-based planning can put planning tools in the hands of staff to make them effective planners where planning might otherwise not take place. Operations planning outlines how the interpretive plan will be implemented. The reality is that the most effective approach is the one that is right for your project and may even combine elements of all those that have been mentioned. The balance of this book will suggest a planning model that incorporates strengths from the varied approaches to help create a process suitable for the plan that needs to be completed.

Exercises

1. Outline a planning approach and some of the methods you have seen used for an interpretive project.

2. What approach discussed in this chapter most closely resembles the one you've outlined? How are they similar? How are they different?

3. List the five things you currently think are the most important to successful interpretive planning. When you finish this book, revisit the list and see if your assumptions have changed. When you finish your first interpretive planning process, review the list again. Continue revising the list as you gain experience.

4. What is the best interpretive planning approach? Explain your answer in an article of about 1,500 words, then submit it to *The Interpreter* or a similar publication.

Interpretation shows up in many places. Like the titles of various planning documents, the various types of facilities where interpretation plays a major role often have names that are used interchangeably even though they may provide very different programs and services. For the purposes of this book, a number of these facilities have been identified with their similarities and differences noted. Note that it is not the size, shape, or location that defines any of these facilities, but rather their function and target markets. All of them can benefit from interpretive planning.

Types of Facilities

Nature Center

The typical nature center is a community-based, not-for-profit organization. Many nature centers are 501(c)3 corporations, governed by a board of directors, while others are a part of local government agencies. The mission statements of most nature centers include educating the public about local or global environmental issues to promote a conservation ethic. Many nature centers focus on stories related to local flora and fauna to help people understand their role in nurturing a healthy environment. Some nature centers use live animals in exhibits and programming, some have active wildlife rehabilitation programs, and still others have policies against holding any live animals for any purpose. Most nature centers provide exhibits and walk-in programming to attract the general public in addition to offering scheduled programs for special groups.

Environmental-Education Center

Environmental-education centers differ from nature centers in one important aspect. Though the ownership and management of EE centers may be similar to that described for nature centers, they are more likely to be affiliated with a university or municipal school district. The typical EE center offers programming designed to complement a science-based curriculum, focusing on biological sciences and related social sciences. Although EE centers are often associated with schools and provide scheduled programs for that market segment, they usually have some aspects (trails, shops, or exhibits, for example) that are open to the public.

Interpretive Center

An interpretive center is often found in a park environment. Its usual function is to provide a central location for communicating a specific theme and introducing important stories to visiting public who are interested in learning more about available resources. Consequently, it may not be located in the most prominent or easily accessed area of the park, but it usually offers a direct visual or physical link to the resource. Most interpretive centers contain a variety of interpretive media, often including exhibits, audiovisual programs, resource libraries, observation areas, and trailheads. Venues for staging interpretive programs are often incorporated into the interpretive center.

Visitor Center

The visitor center performs a slightly different function than the interpretive center, although the two terms are often used interchangeably, or one facility might serve both functions. The visitor center is usually designed to provide services for visitors that might include admissions, restrooms, pay telephones, sales items, and emergency assistance or other amenities. The visitor center often serves as a park's administrative headquarters. Interpretive efforts are generally limited to small lobby exhibits or signs around the outside of the building.

Information Center

The function of the information center is often integrated into the interpretive center or visitor center. If standing alone, the information center is usually a small facility where visitors can find written instructions, maps, and brochures. Information centers are often staffed by a single individual who can provide answers to visitor questions, but may also be "self-service" facilities. Information centers generally do not include interpretive media other than brochures, pamphlets, and books, but the staff person or volunteer on duty is frequently a trained interpreter.

Any or all of these facilities might be found within a park, camp, zoo, or botanical garden or be part of a nature center or historical venue.

Where Does it Fit in the Big Picture?

Any organization or agency with a mandate for informal communications with its publics needs an interpretive plan. Few sites will be caught without a master plan—everyone seems to understand why a master plan is important. However, one of the keys to management success is public perception. Favorable public perception can be enhanced with attractive, efficient, and effective interpretation. That kind of interpretation most often results from a thoughtful interpretive planning process. Generally, organizational goals include imparting some understanding of what the organization is all about. Those goals can be supported by a section in the master plan either calling for or including the interpretive plan. If the interpretive plan is a part of the master plan, then it usually has a better chance for recognized status and a prominent place in the organization's operations. Action plan or operations plan steps should reinforce that place and be accorded appropriate priorities as set forth in the master plan.

What Planning Can Do

Taking part in a planning process can be an eye-opener. Often, managers or interpreters may hold the belief that planning takes too long, is too expensive, or isn't necessary. The temptation is to fall into the trap of seeking the easiest, least expensive, most common solutions for interpretive challenges, usually resulting in uninspired, ineffective, or unimplemented media. However, the planning process often reveals new information that leads to more creative or effective solutions, stimulating innovative ways of thinking that might never have been explored without going through the process. Those individuals involved in the process have an opportunity to express their opinions and generate fresh ideas, making for a more productive workplace.

Planning helps pinpoint issues of concern. The problem you thought you had might not be the one that needs to be solved. For example, let's say your nature center has decided it needs a new visitor contact station near the entry because visitors aren't able to navigate through its maze of roadways to find various program areas. The director has hired a professional planning and design firm to help determine what interpretive features the visitor contact station should have. Through the course of the planning process, it becomes apparent that the real need is to rethink the circulation and signing systems, rather than creating an expensive new facility that visitors are unlikely to use. With this new option, other opportunities begin to materialize throughout the site. By thoughtful planning, you've just saved your nature center over a million dollars in construction fees. With half that amount, you can refurbish existing facilities, improve the circulation and signing systems, and create new programs that are more responsive to your visitor's needs and desires.

The planning process should expose any concerns about the environmental or historical integrity of a site. Does the restoration of an old water plant for a science center require an investigation of hazardous materials? Does turning a cattle ranch into an environmental education center raise the question of arsenic leaching through groundwater toward a planned fishing pond from an old cattle dip site? Where is that smell of gasoline fumes coming from in the basement of the old building being restored for a new museum? Are the stories being told about the resource based on fact or one of the common myths told about the area's history? Environmental and cultural assessments are costly and often reveal painful results. But they are nothing compared to what the public reaction can be to the headlines "Fish Kill in Nature Center Pond Result of Toxic Waste" or "George Washington Never Slept Here."

Planning helps unveil complexities of the issues at hand. It identifies solutions to problems and allows a more-efficient allocation of operational resources, during the planning process and after implementation. A thoughtful planning process forces a manager to look at financial, facility, and staffing strengths and weaknesses to determine what's possible with existing resources or what improvements will be necessary to accomplish projects. Consequently, the plan provides important budget information for future planning and development.

Planning provides short-term goals and objectives to move toward the bigger picture. These goals and objectives help the manager to monitor progress and success. The process often identifies personnel or organizational problems that would ultimately foil any implementation until the immediate problems are handled. The process also provides long-term guidance in a framework for the future. Commitment to a long-range plan ensures that everyone continues to work toward a common goal, regardless of staff changes, financial fallout, or other setbacks along the way. But rigidity should be tempered with judgment. No plan is cast in stone, and all plans should be evaluated and updated periodically (at least every three to five years) to ensure that they reflect current trends, acquisitions, funding strategies, and management styles.

Having a plan in hand saves many agencies from accepting unwanted or undesirable donations of collections or other items that don't fit or directly oppose the organization's mission. Not every Texas nature center should have a polar bear mount in its collection. In fact, probably none of them should. Interpretive plans can spell out a collections policy that should be periodically reviewed, just like the plan, as notions of appropriateness change. Years ago, human bones were often displayed but are now being returned to representatives of the culture for appropriate interment. Live animals or taxidermied mounts, appropriately displayed in some venues, may be looked on as detrimental to public relations in other places.

Planning can often revitalize existing interpretive media. Dated interpretive exhibits can be injected with new life by revising text and updating photos and graphics. A variety of techniques have been used to give old projects new looks, messages, and appeal. Such efforts may save funds and preserve projects with long-established management and local citizen support. Conversely, the plan can also point out when refurbishing custom built exhibits is not in the best interest of the organization because it would be less costly and produce a more effective message if an entirely new approach is taken.

The plan document makes an excellent fund-raising tool. An attractively packaged and well-documented process is extremely appealing to potential donors. A simple executive summary of the plan or an interpretive prospectus based on the plan document provides the basis for grant proposals.

Perhaps most importantly, a good plan is the first step in creating happy customers. Though visitors may never see the plan document, they are the beneficiaries of the plan's implementation. If adequate attention is paid to visitor desires in the planning process, the results reflect positively on the organization in the customer's eyes.

What Planning Cannot Do

While good planning accomplishes many things, it's important to realize that there are some things that planning simply cannot do. Plans do not make things happen. People make things happen, and a good plan makes it easier for that to take place. Often, a plan sits on the shelf collecting dust once it's completed. Though that might be an appropriate place for an unworkable plan, many good plans also die due to a lack of commitment to implementation. It's not the plan's fault if nobody chooses to use it. Many managers are unfamiliar with the appropriate implementation and updating of both short-term and long-range plans, either sticking rigidly to every word or ignoring the entire thing. Neither approach is the most effective use of the dynamic nature of planning. So, rather than evaluating and periodically refreshing their plan, they simply throw it out and start over or worse yet, claim that the planning process doesn't work anyway, so why bother?

Planning cannot guarantee quality of results. In most cases, planning for interpretation is only the first of three steps. The next two are design and construction (usually called fabrication if referring to exhibits or signs). It's not unusual for one individual or group of people to prepare a plan, then have it delivered to a second group for design and possibly even a third group for construction. Every time the plan changes hands through this process, changes are made or the interpretation of the plan differs. The planner no longer has control over the original ideas, especially if the planner is left out of the latter two steps. Often, the changes are not for the better, but are made in the interest of time, money, individual tastes, or other considerations. By the time a building or exhibit gets built, it may not achieve the objectives originally intended by the planner and so will be less effective.

To ensure that your plan accomplishes all that it can, get buy-in from as many individuals as possible. Without the ownership of management and relevant customer groups, the best of interpretive plans have little likelihood of being implemented, no matter how well the planners themselves like their work. A valuable strategy is to communicate with management and customer groups on a regular basis and when appropriate, to include them on the planning team. However, the planner should be prepared for the inevitable conflict that will arise when a well-meaning manager or content expert insists on doing things a certain way in spite of the fact that what he or she wants to do will render the interpretive efforts less effective. Effective interpretation, being both art and science, is filled with subtleties that some people without interpretive training simply do not grasp. Trying to wrestle these people to the ground over the issue is usually not productive. The planner should attempt to educate, using research findings to support his or her argument whenever possible, compromise to salvage important points, and move on to other things.

The Planning Team

Planning is rarely successful when done in a vacuum. The process usually requires input from a number of people, but each organization treats planning differently. Many agencies rely on their interpretive staff to address any and all interpretive planning needs. Although this approach may be valid for individual programs or activities, few field interpreters have specific training in the many varied aspects of interpretive master planning. Being an interpreter and being an interpretive planner require two different skill sets, although they both require a thorough understanding of interpretive principles. In fact, the best interpretive planners are those with some field experience as a front-line interpreter or visitor center manager in addition

Focus groups participate in a planning effort at Midewin National Tallgrass Prairie by voting for their favorite ideas following a brainstorming session. Each participant is given ten votes with instructions to place no more than four votes on any one item. Higher priority items rise to the top while undesirable ideas sift out.

to their planning experience, because that background will give them a better understanding of how what they plan can be implemented and maintained. Since few agencies have experienced interpretive planners on staff, most will hire professional planning firms to fulfill their planning needs with input from staff at all levels.

Determining which approach is right for a particular agency depends on circumstances surrounding the job at hand. Outside help from a professional planning firm is particularly desirable when staff time or ability is limited. However, it would be a mistake to hire a planning firm and then not participate fully in the process. An outside firm provides fresh ideas that may be overlooked by those too close to the everyday operations of the site. Complex projects that require facilitation of public input or multi-agency partnerships often benefit from the third-party objectivity of a professional planning firm. If an organization lacks a graphics shop, an outside firm's expertise in preparing quality presentation graphics can be critical to the success of fund-raising efforts.

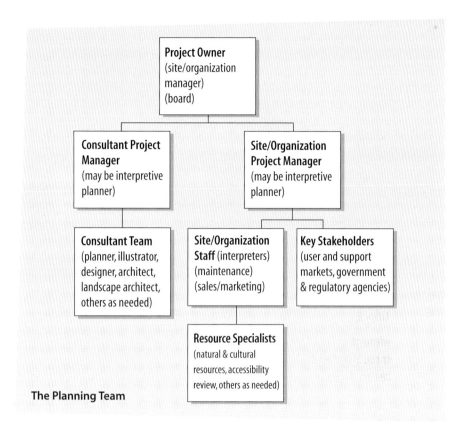

The Planning Team

Regardless of the individual agency's approach to planning, it is important that a project manager be appointed to keep the process moving forward in a positive way. The project manager must be given the authority to call meetings, order changes, contact any outside specialists, and ensure that all those involved in the process are performing their assigned duties. The project manager should also be responsible for designating a planning team that brings all levels of site staff into the process in appropriate ways.

The site manager, director, and/or board must hold responsibility for authorization and approval of draft submittals and final decisions. These individuals must be actively involved or kept abreast of the planning process at all checkpoints. Without their approval, the planning team runs the risk of inappropriate decision-making along the way, resulting in a plan that will never be implemented. However, individuals at these top management levels rarely have interpretive backgrounds or fully understand the implications of

Need Professional Help?

Do:

- Look for a professional planning firm that specializes in interpretive projects.

- Look for a firm with staff members experienced in interpretive master planning.

- Ask if the firm is a commercial member of the National Association for Interpretation (NAI).

- Ask if individual planners are NAI-certified.

- Check references of all bidders. Call their recommended references and others (even some of the ones that they don't necessarily recommend contacting) on their project list.

- Check references on individuals, as well as investigating the company's reputation.

- Look for potential bidders in NAI's Green Pages Directory and *Legacy* magazine.

- Advertise for large projects in the *Commerce Business Daily*.

- Call other site managers or interpreters who have recently completed planning projects for suggestions on potential contractors.

Don't:

- Think things will be different for you if you've gotten word that a particular firm or individual is difficult to work with or inexperienced with interpretive planning.

- Hire architecture or landscape architecture firms without specific interpretive expertise for interpretive planning projects, even if they've done other interpretive projects. (Just because they've done them doesn't mean they've done them well.)

- Hire exhibit fabrication firms for interpretive planning projects.

Though architecture, landscape architecture and exhibit fabrication firms may be skilled at their specialty areas, their lack of understanding of interpretation principles and practicalities of running sites that provide visitor services may come back to haunt you. Insist that they include a skilled interpretive planner as a subcontractor if they don't have one on staff.

TIM MERRIMAN

good interpretive programming. Here's where the interpretive staff makes an important contribution.

The site's interpretive staff are most closely in tune with visitor needs and desires. Front-line interpreters must be tapped for input into the plan if they are not wholly responsible for planning. The paradox is that these interpreters are usually the busiest people at any site and rarely have time to contribute to the process unless specifically directed to do so. In these instances, hiring an outside firm may be the most efficient use of resources, since the firm's planners can facilitate the process and get appropriate input in small bites of time. Once the plan is completed, implementation usually becomes the responsibility of the interpretive staff with support from management.

Whether the team comes from in-house staff talent or draws on the expertise of an outside planning firm, an effective planning team requires representation from all those who will be affected by implementation of the plan. This approach builds ownership in the plan's contents, helping to ensure successful implementation. To assign a single individual the responsibility for developing the interpretive plan misses the tremendous opportunity a team can bring to the table—input from a wide variety of sources and the creative dynamic of a team working together.

Answering the following questions might help you construct the ideal team for your interpretive planning project:

Industrial sites often make good examples of Pine and Gilmore's Experience Economy Theory. The Wooden Shoe Factory in Holland, Michigan, demonstrates the making of wooden shoes (left), then sells the shoes and other thematic souvenirs in its shop.

- Do you have anyone with interpretive planning experience on staff who can enjoyably and effectively lead the process?

- Do you have staff with subject-matter and site expertise who can assist in the planning process and serve as reviewers?

- Who can represent customers by virtue of their daily contact with customer activity at the site and understanding of the region in which they are operating?

- Who are the key stakeholders? Who holds the power, influence, and authority to make the plan happen?

- Who can review the plan for adherence to universal accessibility guidelines?

- Who can speak for management relative to budgeting, maintenance, and staffing and keep the planning process based in operational reality?

- Will outside consultants be an important part of the process? Do you need technical expertise not available on staff?

The interpretive planner may pull the lion's share of the assignment on any planning team but having regular input and review from the others will prove invaluable and help avoid costly oversights.

Customer Input into the Planning Process

The above team members can ensure management's input and buy-in to the interpretive planning process, but that's only part of the support needed. To complete the development of support, customer input to the interpretive planning process can be just as vital. Public input can be as simple as holding a review meeting at the end of the planning process to leading an interagency and public team through a series of workshops to develop the interpretive plan. Several effective ways to solicit customer input include:

- Scheduling public input meetings at critical points in the planning process, including the draft review and final review. Care should be taken to show where input has been incorporated and explanation given when customer input has not been followed.

- Inviting a select group of reviewers (focus groups) from publics that might become participants in or supporters of your implemented interpretive operation. Definite inclusions should be neighborhood representatives, an access-group consultant, members of groups who use your facilities for meetings, and representatives from the schools and academic community.

- Inviting "pencil testing" from among existing customers where the customers role play through the interpretive plan by walking a proposed trail with prototype signs or children play a proposed exhibit game. If planning a children's museum or activity, work with local schools to have an age-appropriate class make suggestions or test ideas.

- Requesting customer response to creative-planning questionnaires. At Riding Mountain National Park in Canada, visitors were invited to design their ideal visitor center by selecting the features and exhibits they thought were most important and placing those features on an outline of the building. When the building was full, they were done.

This process helped identify the relative importance of features and their placement from the customer perspective.

- Building a list of reviewers who will receive mailings of plan phases and will then mail in comments. Several large park agencies have used this process to gain comment from broad population bases.

Managing Public Input

Public input is threatening to many planners. When one agency was asked why the local community's input was not being sought, the response was that they might have to do something about the community's desires if they allowed those desires to be expressed. It's true that public input is often unpredictable and can become hostile to the process if the perception develops that input is not being taken seriously. Careful planning is essential to get the most benefit from public input. Some suggestions that will help in obtaining meaningful input include:

- Use incentives or rewards for participating in the process. Serve dinner or snacks to draw enthusiastic participants or provide free tickets to a special grand opening of the project.

- Maintain contact throughout the process. Some planners produce periodic newsletters or contribute to the organization's membership newsletter throughout the planning process to keep the public informed of progress on the plan.

- Have a means of reporting input that is being gained and how it is being treated. Don't ignore any suggestions. Some contributions may require a sense of humor to respond to but be aware that a seemingly ridiculous suggestion might have been given in all seriousness. If information is gathered at one meeting, show how that information was applied at the next meeting.

- Publish names of contributors or otherwise acknowledge all participants unless they request anonymity.

- Make your requests for input clear. The best way to avoid inappropriate comments or behavior from participants is to say right up front what you and they should expect from the process. For example, you might mention that you are simply gathering information that will have to be filtered through operational realities before a decision can be made about whether to incorporate it into the final plan or not.

Soliciting Input through Meetings

Think about the last time you were in a meeting you actually enjoyed. Hard to picture? Meetings can be little more than facilitated frustration, or they can be highly productive sessions that move the process forward in meaningful ways. Usually, the difference depends on the person in charge of the meeting. For some processes, a true facilitator may be required as described by Roger Schwarz in *The Skilled Facilitator*. Schwarz describes several models for facilitation and suggests that true facilitators maintain an objective distance from the content of the meeting. They simply provide and monitor a group process for the purpose of producing desired results. Schwarz' facilitative consultant is the role most often assumed by interpretive planners. The facilitative consultant provides process but also contributes to content based on his or her previous experience.

Either role can be effective, but only if the meeting leader determines which role he or she intends to play (completely objective or contributing to content) and stays within the confines of that role during the meeting. Facilitators who decide to enter the discussion halfway through the meeting can easily derail the process and alienate planning team members. Facilitative consultants are usually skilled at straddling the fence between letting the group project its own ideas and keeping the meeting on a productive path, all the while interjecting useful bits of information that might influence the outcome of the process.

A good example of the different styles might be to compare a strategic planning consultant and an interpretive planning consultant (though some individuals are equally skilled as both strategic and interpretive planners). Generally, a strategic planning session should be facilitated by an outside source who simply guides the process and stays out of the content generated by the group. An interpretive planning consultant, on the other hand, is generally obligated to guide his or her clients in process and content, because he or she has been hired to provide expertise on all aspects of interpretation. In any case, the facilitator makes a contract with the group and should honor whichever role is most appropriate for the task at hand.

Meetings can be a valuable source of information about the significance of natural or cultural/historic resources, availability of subject matter experts, safety issues, access concerns, the future of views and vistas, use of facilities, community concerns, environmental or architectural concerns, desires for interpretive experiences, thematic messages, and a host of other issues.

Before you hold a meeting, be sure you know what you want to get out of it. Determine the desired outcomes of the session and discuss the

TIM MERRIMAN

Interpretive planning is a collaborative effort that often requires discussions with landscape architects, architects, exhibit designers, resource specialists, and others. At the Wolong Breeding Center for Pandas in Sichuan, China, Lisa Brochu (pictured) facilitated planning sessions that included landscape architect Jim Brighton (pictured), program specialist Sarah Blodgett, National Association for Interpretation Executive Director Tim Merriman, interpretive specialist and translator Jasmine Wei-Li Chen, project manager Tom Lamb, and Professors Fu and Feng, the world's leading panda experts. Input sessions included keepers, administrators, maintenance workers, gardeners, and program specialists from Wolong and other panda breeding centers.

objectives with the group at the beginning of the session so everyone knows where you're headed. Prepare an agenda, but don't assign specific times to the various elements. Although you'll need to keep track of your time to ensure that you accomplish your meeting objectives, participants may feel pressured to adhere to published time blocks that need to flex depending on the group dynamic. A better approach is to list the major items that need to be accomplished and ask if there are others before you get started. During the meeting, if you find the group straying from agenda items, bring them back on track quickly, but offer to put the item that's grabbing their attention on a "parking lot" to be addressed at another time so that the issue is captured and the participants feel they've been heard.

Invite participants from a broad spectrum of the community and agencies involved, especially those who have concerns about the process.

Attempt to get input from anticipated market segments from outside the local area if possible. Make sure you assign someone to take notes during the meeting. After the meeting, make copies of the notes for those in attendance. Distribute the notes and ask if anyone remembers anything differently. These written notes will form the basis for some of your planning decisions so it's important for them to be accurate and for everyone on the planning team to be in agreement that they are accurate. It's a good idea to ask for signatures on the meeting notes to ensure that everyone's on the same page.

Use the meeting as an opportunity to educate the public about the project and its implications, but don't underestimate the intelligence of those who have been invited to participate. Although few may understand the finer points of interpretation, most know far more than the planner about other issues relevant to the project. To bring everyone to common ground, start the meeting by defining interpretation and describing the interpretive planning process. Meetings will be more productive if the entire group understands the point of the project and how interpretation can be used to create intellectual and emotional connections.

Carefully consider and consolidate comments, or use an adapted nominal group process to clarify, combine, and prioritize comments. Brainstorming allows group members to get many ideas expressed, but too often the planner stops there and does not allow the group to come to any conclusions about the brainstormed ideas. Disney calls this the "blue-sky phase," where no ideas are bad ideas. Depending on your goal as a planner, you might want to take the following steps (adapted from Corky McReynolds, Director of Treehaven Field Station) to encourage the group to narrow their focus:

1. **Brainstorming ideas.** Allow people to say whatever comes in their head related to the question at hand and record it on an easel pad. If some people tend to hang back, encourage a "round robin" approach, asking each individual in turn for an idea until everyone has contributed all they can.

2. **Clarifying ideas.** Read each comment and ask if anyone in the group requires clarification of the idea before proceeding. This is an important step and although most groups will rarely ask for clarification of individual items in this step, as the next step begins to take shape, they discover they really did need clarification after all.

3. **Combining ideas.** Check for similarities between comments. If there are comments that can be combined satisfactorily because they are

simply different ways of saying the same thing, mark them as having been combined. This step helps refine the list so that the next step remains undiluted.

4. **Prioritizing ideas.** Give each participant a total of ten votes. Allow each one to vote on his or her top choices, placing up to four votes on one item. Participants can distribute their ten votes in any manner they wish, as long as they don't use more than four on any one item. To make this step a little easier, use small stickers (dots or stars) cut into groups of ten. Participants enjoy the activity involved in placing the stickers next to their favored responses (especially if the stickers have cute faces or shapes) and the stickers make it easier to tally the results.

    Almost always, this procedure identifies four or five top ideas that can then be acted upon in whatever manner is most appropriate. The remaining ideas don't necessarily disappear. They simply don't take as high a priority for the planning team. This "ten/four" process can help winnow out ideas that are inappropriate for whatever reason. It also allows you as the planner to address the fact that the group process helps determine how the plan goes ahead, not any one individual's personal agenda.

Regardless of the process used, all comments gathered during meetings should be given a fair hearing. If the comments will be rejected, be prepared to document the reasons for the rejection. Include references to the input and decision-making process in the plan document. If appropriate, it might also be wise to indicate ideas that were considered but rejected so that the plan cannot be refuted later if someone feels that inadequate input was considered.

No matter how skilled a facilitator the planner may be, some contentious issues simply will not go away. Understand that there may be situations where trying to achieve consensus may actually be more destructive than what may be construed as arbitrary decision-making on the part of administrators. The parking lot provides one avenue for deferring discussions that will derail the process. If it's one individual who is simply not going to agree to anything or be a team player, it may be necessary to remove that person from the process, obtaining their input separately from the rest of the group. Good facilitators need to think on their feet during meetings, to be open to new ways of doing things and to finding creative solutions in difficult situations, but be realistic. Not everyone gets what they want all the time. Sometimes the best a facilitator can do is keep the group from imploding while the group comes to that realization on its own.

Exercises

1. Interview an agency planner. Talk about their approach to planning teams and how they integrate interpretive planning into overall planning efforts. What methods do they use for gathering public input?

2. Outline a planning project, then prepare a list of potential bidders from professional planning firms. Use at least three sources to complete your list and list at least six potential bidders.

3. Set up a planning team for the project outlined in Exercise 2 with yourself as project manager. Create an organizational chart that shows each member of your team. List each member's role and responsibilities. Discuss how you will keep the team on track and moving forward during the project, including how you will handle disagreements among the various members.

4. Prepare a set of interview questions that could be used to determine a company's potential for successful completion of the project outlined in Exercise 2.

5. Read at least two books on the art of meeting facilitation.

What makes a good interpretive planner? Is planning a skill that can be learned or is it based on some ethereal intuition? The answer is, of course, that it depends . . . on the situation, on the individual, on the desired results, and on any number of other variables. Almost anyone can follow a series of basic planning steps and come up with a plan, if "plan" is defined simply as a way to get from Point A to Point B. But in fact, not everyone is cut out to be a planner. Some people are unwilling, or unable, to look beyond formulaic planning and investigate creative options that may yield better results. So there are planners, and then there are *good* planners.

Some good planners are simply born that way. From an early age, they are able to process information in a way that leads to successful outcomes. Planning comes as naturally to them as breathing because it's just a part of their nature. These people seem to exhibit an intuitive grasp of the big picture that may elude others who either get bogged down in or completely ignore details. Natural planners tend to have problem-solving personalities that put details in reasonable perspective.

If you don't seem to fit that personality profile, don't despair. Like interpretation, planning is a skill that can be taught to a certain degree, if the training recipient is open to finding new ways of looking at things. Several universities offer coursework in planning. To find the universities that offer interpretive courses and related planning courses, check with the National Association for Interpretation, which maintains a guide to universities and colleges with interpretive curricula. NAI and other professional organizations also offer training workshops from time to time. NAI's Certified Interpretive Planner program includes a five-day, hands-on workshop. On-the-job training can often be found through internships with a variety of federal, state, and local agencies. You might also offer to apprentice yourself to an established, self-employed interpretive planner, but understand that most self-employed individuals make just enough money to support themselves and may be reluctant to take on an inexperienced assistant who's unwilling to work for little or no financial reward initially.

How to Recognize a Good Interpretive Planner

Valid credentials in this field can be difficult to come by. Certainly, a good planner should have some educational exposure to the principles of interpretation. The best planners also have at least a nodding acquaintance with the fields of marketing, architecture, landscape architecture, park planning and management, urban planning and design, interior design, exhibit design, graphic design, social psychology, communications, computer technology, biology, anthropology, geology, and business administration. Certainly, it's not required that the interpretive planner be an expert in any of these fields, but interpretive planners may be called upon to work with or provide analysis of all of these areas as they relate to an interpretive project, so they should at least understand the basic vocabulary of each.

Field experience as an interpreter or visitor center manager or comparable job description adds to the body of knowledge upon which an interpretive planner can draw; however, being an interpreter does not equate with being an interpretive planner. The two areas share some background knowledge, but require different skills. Likewise, the interpretive planner is not expected to be an expert in any particular subject matter (such as botany), but he or she should be able to research any subject area and be able to converse appropriately with subject matter experts on a given project.

The best credential is experience as an interpretive planner and lots of it. Years of experience expose the planner to a variety of situations and individuals. The best planners learn something new every day and are able to maintain a fresh approach and attitude no matter what the circumstances.

In 1998, NAI instituted a certification process for recognizing qualified interpretive planners. This process involves a testing component as well as a performance component to determine whether an individual has the basic skills to be recognized as an interpretive planner. To qualify for the certification process, one must have either an academic background related to interpretive planning or at least four years experience as a planner.

No matter what their credentials, the best planners are those who are able to balance their approach to planning. The planning process requires logical left-brain analysis that stimulates the right brain to come up with ideas for successful accomplishment of stated objectives. If the planner's personality is heavily weighted toward the left brain, he or she may become mired in logical solutions that may look good on paper but be unrealistic in the field. Worse yet, these people tend to fall prey to the "analysis paralysis" syndrome, logically laying out the challenges but never coming to a conclusion about how to resolve a particular issue. On the other hand (or other brain), right-brainers tend to skip analysis altogether and head right for the design drawing board without thinking through all the implications of their ideas or if an idea is even appropriate for a particular situation, usually resulting in wasted time and money further down the line.

A good interpretive planner will never have the "right" answer, or the only answer for any given situation. Maintaining a self-righteous attitude means that at least a dozen other possible solutions are undoubtedly being overlooked. A good planner will recognize the ability to view situations from any number of angles as a strength rather than a failing of the interpretive planning process and be prepared to suggest the *most effective* answer for the situation. Furthermore, the good planner will be able to explain why the selected option is the most effective approach based on the findings of previous analyses.

As frustrating as it may be at times, a good interpretive planner will answer almost every question with, "It depends," and then follow through with a thoughtful process that defines the variables. Because every situation is different and requires different approaches, the good planner remains flexible in process and products, matching both to the challenges at hand instead of relying on cookie-cutter responses.

Good planners are often considered visionaries. They are able to see beyond the "what is" to the "what if" and figure out a way to make that happen. They look at an apple and see the orchard, the processing plant, the grocery store, and tonight's dessert. In other words, they see relationships and connect little pieces into an overall puzzle, often called "the big picture." Freeman Tilden touched on this concept with his fifth principle of interpretation in *Interpreting Our Heritage* when he said, "Interpretation should aim to present a whole rather than a part, and must address itself to the whole man rather than any phase." It is this quality that is often lacking in inexperienced planners and it is a difficult one to teach. Like the intuition that blesses a natural planner, the ability to see beyond the obvious is almost innate. Some successful ways to broaden the planning

NAI's Certified Interpretive Planner classes are offered at a variety of sites. This class worked on the Asian Giant exhibit at the Dallas Zoo.

perspective and enable the planner to incorporate a more holistic way of thinking are discussed in later chapters.

Good planners are ethical, but are not above what is known in the business as "creative thievery." Planners should never take credit for someone else's ideas or work, but there's nothing wrong with looking at the efforts of others and improving their concept to create something new. Every time a planner enters an interpretive facility or site, he or she should be taking mental notes, asking, "How can this be better?" In this way, the planner sharpens his or her own skills while not intruding on the work of others. One of the best ways to learn what works and what doesn't is to engage in visitor observation wherever you go and then analyze your findings to come up with new ways of solving problems you've observed. What you discover may come in handy for your next planning scenario.

Finally, good planners must have at heart Tilden's "essential ingredient" in every phase of their work. They must genuinely love what they do, for without that commitment and the enthusiasm it generates, the planning

TIM MERRIMAN

Field work helps the planner understand implications of management, markets, message, mechanics so that the most effective media can be determined. When planner Lisa Brochu and US-China Environmental Fund president Marc Brody viewed a project site at the International Friendship Forest at the Great Wall of China, they learned more about what interests visitors at the site. Note that a good planner never leaves home without something to take notes on.

effort will be mediocre at best and nothing short of disastrous at worst. Ralph Waldo Emerson summed it up when he said, "Nothing great is ever achieved without enthusiasm."

Career Options in Interpretive Planning

If you're thinking of interpretive planning as a primary career choice, there are a number of opportunities for plying your trade. Because interpretive planning should be a required part of every job related to interpretation, some of the most likely places to look are agencies and organizations that manage interpretive sites. Individual interpretive sites like a single park, museum, or nature center, tend to avoid hiring full-time interpretive planners who have no other marketable skills that can be used when planning projects are complete. Sites like these will usually contract for planning projects. Although this approach may seem somewhat short-sighted since planning should be an ongoing process, it is nevertheless the way most such sites operate. Generally, agencies that will be responsible for multiple planning projects over an extended period of time have a higher potential for hiring full-time planners. Be advised that many of these agencies hire from within, drawing their "planners" from a pool of employees that may have little or no actual planning experience. Again, this approach may be considered short-sighted, but it is a reality for many agencies who are unaware of the potential that skilled planners can bring to their organization.

Another career option for interpretive planners is to work for a planning and design or exhibit company. The NAI Green Pages directory listed twenty-two interpretive planning and design companies in 2002. In reality, few of these companies had interpretive planning expertise on staff and were primarily design or fabrication firms. Since the definition of interpretive planning is often unclear, these firms are not necessarily misrepresenting themselves; however, they also do not provide planning, either having to subcontract that skill or just skipping straight to design instead, often creating more problems than solutions. If you choose to seek employment with a company that offers "interpretive planning and design," you should ask the following questions:

- Does the firm do any other kind of work besides providing services for interpretive sites (designing apartment buildings, providing directional signs for shopping malls, etc.)? If so, how much of your time will be devoted to these types of projects and how much to interpretive sites?

- Will you be responsible for bringing in interpretive contracts? If so, how much of the company's marketing strategy and what duties will you be responsible for?

- How does the firm handle the interaction of planners and designers? Of planners and fabricators?

- What specific projects has the firm worked on in the past three years?

- Does the firm belong to NAI as a commercial member?

- Are any of the firm's employees certified by NAI or other professional organizations?

- What salary and benefits are available?

Before committing to a particular firm, it would be advisable to check with their previous clients to decide if their creative philosophy and approach to handling clients are compatible with yours. Since planning is both a left- and right-brain endeavor, feeling frustrated and stifled in a company setting that doesn't share your planning philosophy is a very real possibility. On the other hand, established companies often offer employment benefits and starting salaries around $20,000 to $40,000 with the potential to range up to $60,000 or more after several years. The security of a regular paycheck may be short-lived however, since the market for interpretive planning services (or a lack thereof) may require occasional layoffs.

If entrepreneurship is in your blood and you are an accomplished interpretive planner with a good network of contacts in the field, self-employment is always a possibility. Interpretive planning can be an extremely low overhead venture, requiring only a computer, a phone, access to printing and binding services, and the ability to travel. The benefits of such self-employment include the potential for working out of your home, setting your own schedule (to the extent that your clients approve), and setting your own rate of pay. But figuring out what that rate of pay is can be tricky. For example, if you know you want to make $40,000 gross in a given year, a common mistake is to plan on working approximately 2,000 hours (full-time) at an hourly rate of $20 per hour. Sounds reasonable, but when you take out self-employment taxes and overhead expenses not reimbursed by your clients, you may find your gross income inadequate for the amount of time required to achieve it.

The reality of self-employment is that only about seventy-five percent of your time can be spent in billable hours. The remaining twenty-five percent is spent on marketing your services, clerical time for filing, bookkeeping, and other chores that seem to keep your desktop piled high. On average, about forty percent of your gross income will be eaten up by taxes and other overhead expenses. So a more appropriate formula for figuring your hourly billable rate (the rate you charge your clients) might be: Desired gross income equals hourly rate multiplied by 1,500 hours (seventy-five percent of full-time or whatever variable amount you decide you want to work) multiplied by overhead multiplier of two and a half. In other words, if you want to gross $60,000 (so that your net will be about $24,000) and you're willing to work full-time, you should be charging at least $40 per billable hour. That formula works, of course, only if you're able to sustain enough billable hours throughout the year, which brings us to the down side of self-employment.

It is highly recommended that anyone making the leap to self-employment, particularly as an interpretive planner, have enough savings to withstand a period of at least twelve months without income from any other source. One of the major drawbacks to being a planner-for-hire is that agencies are rarely set up to pay in advance. Consultants are generally paid when the work is complete, although in-progress payments can and should

TIM MERRIMAN

Interpretive opportunities are everywhere for the planner with vision.

be negotiated. What this means to your bank balance is that you will be required to perform work and expend money on a project for a period of perhaps three to six months. At the end of that period, when the work is complete, you send an invoice. Processing that invoice may take another 30 to 60 days depending on the client. Conceivably, you could begin work in January and not see a dime until August. The self-employed planner must therefore be an expert in juggling several projects at once to stagger the receipt of payments so that groceries can still be a part of everyday life. Before deciding that this lifestyle is the best one for you, talk to several self-employed people, particularly some in this field.

Some companies offer a hybrid existence, allowing you to retain your self-employed status as a contract employee. Depending on the terms of the contractual agreement, this approach can be a mutually beneficial arrangement, but you should check with your tax advisor and an attorney prior to committing yourself.

You should also consider your network of friends and family. You will need their support in many ways, especially as you get your business started.

Make sure they understand what you're getting into and are willing to stand behind your decision with you.

Exercises

1. List five aspects of your personality that would make you a good planner.

2. Interview an NAI-certified interpretive planner. What qualities does he or she exhibit in their approach to planning?

3. Identify three potential employers for interpretive planners. Get information about their salary ranges, benefits, opportunities for advancement, and planning philosophies.

4. Attend an NAI Certified Interpretive Planner workshop and complete the certification requirements.

Once you've established the need for interpretive planning, the question becomes how to get going with some sort of logical process. Each interpretive planner will eventually develop a process with individual variations in emphasis and success of outcomes. There is no single method or set of steps that will guarantee success in every situation. But there are commonalities between projects that allow a simple summary of an effective process made up of the following stages:

4

The Planning

Process

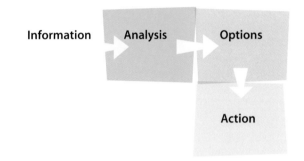

Information   Analysis   Options

Action

This four-stage process overlays the five Ms of management, markets, message, mechanics, and media. In each of the four steps, the five Ms are the elements that must be considered. The Ms are touchstones during the four steps of the process, acting as constant evaluation filters at every step along the way.

Information

Effective planning begins with information. The more you know, the more likely it is that you can develop a plan that addresses the desires of visitors and the needs of management. Information comes from an unlimited number of sources, but can generally be divided into primary or secondary sources. Primary sources provide more direct information because they involve your personal observations or records. For example, you could

Information Needs Checklist

NOTE: Not all items will be applicable to every project. Some projects require additional information not listed here.

Management
- ❑ "Memoranda of Understanding" with other agencies (federal, state, county, local, non-profit groups, etc.) that may affect operations
- ❑ Maintenance system, land-management plan, signage plan
- ❑ Contracts and concessionaires
- ❑ Existing staff levels
- ❑ Planned staff additions/deletions
- ❑ Annual report(s)
- ❑ Budget for last five years
- ❑ Budget sources (both capital and operating)
- ❑ History of capital improvements financing and projects
- ❑ Other sources of funding
- ❑ Easements and other property restrictions
- ❑ History of your organization (when founded, significant growth/changes, etc.)
- ❑ Objectives (interpretive, program, exhibit, building, lands, management)
- ❑ Guidelines or constraints

Markets
- ❑ Demographic profiles for nearest cities and surrounding counties
- ❑ Cooperating association member information package, number and profile of members
- ❑ Promotional materials
- ❑ Who else provides leisure/educational services in what types of complementary and competitive facilities within 100-mile radius
- ❑ Statistics on use of programs and services (profile of users: schools, families, etc.)
- ❑ History with accessible programs (what types, attendance, etc.)
- ❑ Special events (what, when, attendance)

Message
- ❑ Base maps for sites (including topo, surveys, soils/geology, toxic waste sites for county, access)
- ❑ Environmental-assessment information (climate, air quality, water quality, etc.)
- ❑ Vegetation and wildlife checklists, indicate threatened and endangered species
- ❑ Cultural-history information (previous owners of site, archaeological surveys, etc.)

Mechanics
- ❑ Existing facilities/functions, square footage
- ❑ Currently planned facility additions/deletions and square footages required for various functions

Media
- ❑ Delivery system (how are current programs and services delivered to public)
- ❑ List of interpretive resources (slide files, mounts, equipment, etc.)

survey user groups for direct input, have public-input meetings, or use focus groups to provide information about what might be of interest to user or support markets. Or, if your plan will require that a trail be located near the nesting sites of great blue herons, you could spend some time observing rookeries at other locations to determine what the effects of such a trail location might be.

Interviewing individuals with content expertise (paleontologists at a dinosaur dig site or botanists at a native plants garden) can also provide insight. Gathering primary information can be expensive and time-consuming, but there are times when it is the most effective way to find out what you need to know.

Most consultants who have been in business several years have enough experience gathering primary information that they can easily extrapolate relevant information from previous experiences. Their experience with similar situations can be trusted to provide a reliable basis for decision-making.

Secondary information comes from existing documentation. These sources may include previous surveys, staff observations, previous planning efforts, and archival information. In many cases, a search of existing paperwork and a trip to the library or Internet may turn up everything you need to continue the process.

The information you need will vary according to the specific planning project, but if you consider the areas of management, markets, message and mechanics, you'll usually have enough information to lead to appropriate media decisions. The information-needs checklist (page 52) is a good place to start, but remember that the specific items needed for any one project will vary and not all items will be needed for every project.

Generally, the information-gathering stage will be done on-site by agency staff. If you are the agency staff person assigned to gathering information, it's easy to ignore the importance of this step. Often, agency personnel may feel like they already know all there is to know about the project, or don't want to take time to back up and sift through the information, but that would be a mistake. A thorough investigation into the four areas of management, market, message, and mechanics can make the difference between media decisions that are highly effective and media decisions that simply waste money and create problems for the organization.

If you're working with a consultant, ask him or her to gather information, but collecting as much existing documentation as you can will likely save time and dollars. Make copies of all information you're passing to the consultant and flag those items that you want returned when the project ends.

Directional signage can be engaging, fun, and thematic. At Walt Disney World's Animal Kingdom, Rafiki effectively directs traffic around a one-way loop trail.

Analysis

Unfortunately , this step is one of the most frequently overlooked aspects of planning, and yet, it is undoubtedly one of the most important. Analysis of the information gathered goes beyond simply answering the questions of who, what, where, and why. Analysis determines the *implications* of the information, indicating appropriate directions for taking action in light of those implications. With every piece of information gathered, the question should be asked, "What does this mean for the interpretive program?"

For example, let's say a 600-acre natural site is located adjacent to a developing neighborhood with an unusually large proportion of elementary-age schoolchildren. The owners of the natural site want to develop it as an environmental-education facility, but want to cater to corporate executives and land-use agency managers rather than provide services for schoolchildren. Results of a survey of the proposed users indicate that such a facility might be a great idea if it were open to the families of said corporate executives (many of whom live in the adjacent neighborhood), but that they themselves do not have the time or the desire

Never miss an interpretive opportunity. Restroom signs at Walt Disney World's Animal Kingdom relate directly to visitors' experiences, making a connection with the animals featured at the park.

☆THE

SCOOP ON POOP

South American sloths fertilize the trees they live in by depositing their poop at the base of the tree once every eight days.

African elephants hold the record for the **heaviest** poop in one day by a land animal: 300 pounds (136 kg).

Boa constrictors poop only once every 2-3 weeks.

Hippos spin their tails to spread their nutrient-rich poop along river shores, providing nourishment to plants and fish.

to participate in environmental seminars during their work days. Analysis of this information would lead one to believe that the best use of the site might be to respond to the needs of the adjacent landowners and their schools rather than attempting to facilitate meetings that will not be attended by corporate executives. It is never enough to simply gather the information—the careful planner must always analyze the findings and draw conclusions that will lead to more successful results.

How in-depth the analysis needs to be will depend on the individual project. It's helpful to develop analysis tools that can be adapted to a variety of situations. For example, Tim Merriman, executive director of the National Association for Interpretation, suggests using a matrix that places relationship to mission on one axis and relationship to money on the other axis. Adapted from Stephen Covey's original urgency matrix, the money/mission matrix places products, programs, and services in one of four quadrants to provide a graphic representation of how resources are being allocated in the organization. This simple tool often reveals significant disparity between the amount of money associated with an activity and the

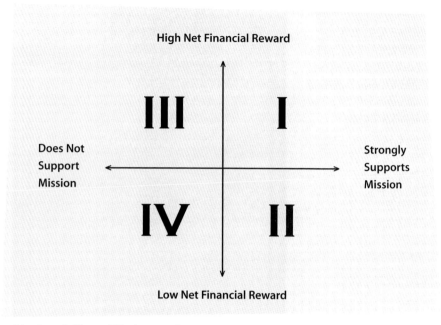

High Net Financial Reward

III   I

Does Not Support Mission   **Strongly Supports Mission**

IV   II

Low Net Financial Reward

Merriman's Money/Mission Matrix

original purpose of the site or agency.

Items that fall within Quadrant IV (low mission relationship; low net financial reward) should simply be stopped until or unless they can be moved into Quadrant I or II through reconfiguring the activity somehow. Items within Quadrant III (low mission relationship, high net reward) should be adapted to better reflect the mission statement, moving them to Quadrant I. Although they may not be too damaging financially, they also don't help the organization to fulfill its purpose. Quadrants I and II are where the organization should strive to place all its programs, products and services. Some items may not be as financially rewarding as others, but if their mission relationship is strong enough, that may be okay. Ideally, a balance will be struck between the low- and high-dollar items to help even things out.

Analysis of the organization's overall budget can also be helpful. Plotting the annual budget and sources of financing using pie charts or graphs is a useful tool to identify problem areas in income or outflow that might affect the overall interpretive program.

Regardless of whether the information collected relates to management, markets, message, mechanics, or media, analyze the implications for interpretation before proceeding to the next step in the process.

Options

Once the information has been analyzed, several solutions to the challenge at hand may become evident. There is rarely only one possible approach to any particular planning challenge and the solutions are virtually endless. Identifying a variety of solutions and listing the advantages and disadvantages of each can help solidify the most appropriate solution. Often, the final decision will not be to select one of the offered solutions, but to combine aspects of several options to come up with a solution that incorporates the best of all possible worlds.

The options phase is where the media "M" usually becomes the star of the show. However, it shouldn't be the only one on stage. Often, new strategies for resolving management, markets, or mechanics issues may arise out of the analysis phase that can cause the planner to rethink the entire operation instead of simply seeking media solutions.

Action

Having determined the most appropriate options to pursue, the planner then lists the specific actions that will lead to the most desirable results. This phase may include media descriptions or written strategies that provide the details about selected options. Generally, an action plan will also be included to indicate what happens next in the process and who's responsible for getting it done so that implementation can take place in a timely fashion. It's a good idea to include costs and a time schedule related to each action item as a reality check and to help monitor progress towards the goal. It may be helpful to place the action plan in a table format. This approach allows the action plan to be removed from the plan document and posted as a checklist, reminding everyone involved in the project of the steps that must take place for successful implementation.

The Process in Review

Generally, the interpretive planner should be the one to craft the written plan based on input from the planning team; however, the planner should turn over the document for review by other team members on a regular basis during the process. This approach allows the planner to make adjustments throughout the process and fine tune the final product.

Reviews by committee can become cumbersome if disagreements exist between team members. To resolve conflicts, the planner must review the source of the problem and present reasonable alternatives for consideration. When the issue cannot be resolved by this method, the planner should defer to whatever management level is required for a final decision. It is important

Bronze sculptures evoke the power and emotion of a buffalo jump at South Dakota's Tatanka: Story of the Bison.

that issues are resolved early on in the interest of saving time and money further down the line. It is easy and inexpensive to make changes in the beginning stages of the process, but as a plan develops, every change will cost significantly more.

If the planner is a consultant and reviews are provided by the client team, it is vital that the client's project manager be responsible for resolving conflicts among review comments before returning the comments to the consultant. The consultant should not try to guess which comments take higher priority when a conflict arises. He or she can provide guidance to the client about which comments may make the most sense, but often internal political realities are at play with conflicting comments and the consultant can get drawn into playing intermediary or having to make assumptions about which comments to accept and which to reject. Neither situation is conducive to a productive process.

Flexibility is a good thing in the planning process and a desired quality in an interpretive planner; however, once the plan document (or part thereof) has been approved, the appropriate action is to move forward. Too

The Museum at Warm Springs' architectural elements reflect the tipi homes of the Warm Springs people. The motif is continued on the entry sign.

often, plans become mired in uncertainty as new people or ideas are brought into the process after critical decisions have already been made. In most of these cases, the plan stalls out, the process becomes unproductive, the team loses interest, and the project dies.

Pitfalls of Planning

Because there are so many variables to consider, discussion of the most appropriate planning process can be disconcertingly vague. It is far easier to discuss common problem areas that many inexperienced planners face. Being aware of the potential pitfalls can help the planner sidestep them throughout the process.

Making assumptions. Good planning is based on factual information. While it is true that intuition plays an important role in the process, the planner should avoid basing decisions on assumptions, particularly about the position of management. Thorough questioning of site staff often reveals hidden agendas that will influence the outcome of a project.

Planning by anecdote. Although sometimes the only information available is based on staff observations or the stories of a single vocal visitor, such limited information usually stunts the outcome of the process. A quick survey or field observations by an objective viewer can often reveal that what really happens on-site is quite different than what is believed to happen on-site.

Jumping to media selection. Gathering information about the management, message, markets, and mechanics provides a solid background for determination of media. If you leave out one of these Ms or figure out media first, chances are good you'll end up having to backtrack or end up with an unsuccessful project.

Forgetting to analyze. Simply listing resources is not the same as analyzing the implications of those resources within the larger context of management, mechanics, market, message, and media.

Ignoring the facts. When careful analysis reveals a mistake about to be made, the planner should provide other alternatives rather than forging ahead with a plan doomed to fail. Be aware that sometimes managers prefer to ignore the facts for a variety of reasons. If that happens, the planner's choices are limited to removing him- or herself from the project, trying to convince the manager to rethink his or her position, or giving in gracefully and going down the wrong road with the best attitude possible. Which choice you make will depend on the circumstances, but generally speaking, option number two (trying to persuade the manager) is the high road, followed by option number three (giving in gracefully) if number two doesn't work out. Option number one (opting out of the project) may make you feel better initially, but the reality is that the project result may turn even worse if you abandon ship, so think hard before choosing this one. Some influence is often better than none at all.

Can you guess what I'm thinking? This game, frequently played by disgruntled managers or employees with a personal agenda, can cost an agency dearly. One nature center director playing this game with an expensive contractor from half a continent away deliberately gave misinformation and withheld critical information, thwarting a major exhibit project and costing his agency over $100,000 in fees set aside for planning and design, all because he had a personal bone to pick with his supervisor. Needless to say, he no longer works for that agency. Sadly, it took years for the agency to recover and move forward with a different exhibit firm.

Ignoring the disabled. Able-bodied planners tend to forget the need for accessibility. If you are able-bodied, rent a wheelchair for a week and try to visit some of your favorite recreation and interpretation sites. Try a few other sites and visit them blindfolded or with soundproof earphones. These quick trips into a different world view don't come close to approximating the daily reality of someone with disabilities, but attempts at considerate planning become obvious fairly quickly. Learn to recognize potential accessibility problems during the planning stages to avoid situations like the visitor center that was totally dependent on sound for all interpretation or the central Texas site that erected metal Braille signs in full sun. Planning a mix of media that makes part of the message available to everyone means no one has to miss out. Check the latest Americans with Disabilities Act (ADA) standards and have your plans reviewed and pencil-tested by a variety of individuals with different physical capabilities to ensure accessibility is appropriately considered.

Not involving boards, special interests, general public. Planners who work in a vacuum usually meet with limited success. No one can be aware of all the ramifications of a single project, much less multiple projects. People who are likely to pay for the project's implementation, and those who are likely to be end users are especially important to include in the process. Special-interest groups may be an important part of your project and should not be ignored. Avoid the attitude of one federal employee who, when planning for a visitor center that would impact Native American basket-material-gathering areas, suggested that it would be inappropriate to talk with tribal representatives, because, "If we ask them, they might tell us what they want, and then we'll have to respond."

Changes after approvals. Once a decision has been made, move forward. Unless there is legitimate reason for taking a backward step (and someone on the planning team just changing his or her mind does not constitute a legitimate reason), it's important to the momentum and the cost of the project to keep on track. The easiest way to avoid changes after approvals is to be sure to include key decision-makers at each step and to have those people physically sign off on documents. Ask for signatures on one of three choices: approved as is, approved with changes as noted, or not approved. This approach should make status of approvals very clear at any point in the project.

Analysis paralysis. Once information has been gathered, it's easy to become overwhelmed. Learn to sift through the information and quickly distill the facts that have implications for your planning project. Don't get distracted by information or issues that have no relevance to your project, but don't get tunnel vision either. Sometimes the information gathering process reveals that the project at hand might need to be rethought in light of a larger background issue. If that is the case, don't spend time trying to salvage the original project. Just leave it to solve the background problem first and you may find that the project you thought you were working on is no longer necessary at all.

Poor packaging. Many a plan has failed simply because it was not taken seriously. Although the look of the document should have no bearing on the quality of the planning effort, it may be difficult to sell supporters on a plan that does not convey its own importance and a sense of excitement by the way it looks. Be aware of who will be reading the document so you can write and format appropriately for its readers.

Function following form. This problem is a frequent complication that occurs when architects design interpretive facilities without the input of an interpretive planner. A good planner should be able to pencil-test architectural plans to ensure that visitors and staff can move through and use the building or site in an appropriate way. Often, the only way to avoid retrofitting or rebuilding a structure is to allow the interpretive plan and visitor experience to drive the facility and site plans. In this manner, the building and site features can not only support the interpretive program, but they can often reinforce the theme and create a higher-quality overall visitor experience. (Remember the fossils incorporated into the walls of the visitor center in the Jurassic Park movie?) Including interpretive planners, architects, and landscape architects on the team from the beginning will help ensure an integrated effort built around function rather than form.

Process vs. Model

The simplified four-stage information-analysis-options-action process described above suggests a logical order in which to proceed through a planning project. But it doesn't provide much direction about what specific items need to be considered throughout the process to ensure success. The remainder of this book suggests a planning model based on the five components that must be considered for a successful plan—management, markets, message, mechanics, and media. Overlaying the 5-M Model onto the four-step process ensures that none of the critical components will be ignored during any phase of the planning process. Each of the five Ms

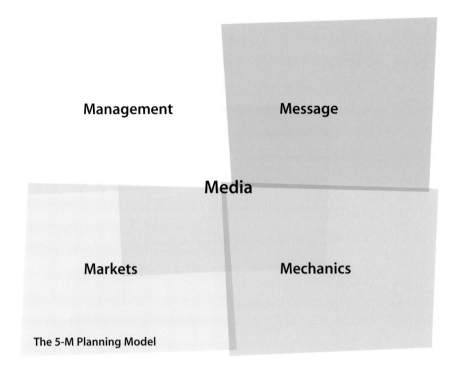

Management   **Message**

Media

Markets   **Mechanics**

The 5-M Planning Model

must be looked at during each of the four steps, but to varying degrees in each step.

The interesting thing about this particular model is that it provides a framework for every interpretive planning project, whether that project involves development of a system-wide interpretive program or is simply a plan for a single exhibit or program effort. Once you commit the model to memory, you will never again forget to consider critical pieces of information that influence the success of your project.

For years, interpretive planning proponents have tried to distill the process into more detailed steps so that anyone could write an interpretive plan if he or she simply followed directions and filled in the blanks. Some planners suggest that filling out forms or holding X number of meetings will leave you with a plan. While this approach may provide a comfort zone for inexperienced planners and often does result in a document that can be called a plan, it does little to create viable solutions to significant planning challenges. If the cookbook method worked, then every site would have cost-effective interpretation that gets every message across to every visitor. But that is rarely the case. More often, a lack of understanding about the variables involved in making the best media choices or even changing the way business is conducted at a site leads to development of interpretation that fails on a number of fronts. The installed interpretive elements end up being a waste of money and time because they simply do not do the job intended. And because they fail, management begins to wonder about the value of any further interpretive efforts. Establishing the value of effective interpretation cannot be overstated—the short-term effect is visitor satisfaction leading to accomplishment of management objectives, but the long-term effect is continued support of the interpretive program, ultimately resulting in greater potential for stewardship of the resource.

The 5-M Model

The 5-M Interpretive Planning Model helps you remember to consider all the components that could influence your media selection. It works because it keeps the planner from ignoring critical information. It is not a recipe. In fact, it's just the opposite. It's simply a list of ingredients. How you choose to combine them and the amounts of each that you include will determine the final outcome. You can take the same milk, flour, sugar, egg, and vanilla and end up with a cake, cookies, waffles, or even French toast. The model offers flexibility in a framework. Use it to create the masterpiece that will most effectively communicate your messages to your audiences.

Although the visual representation of the 5-M Interpretive-Planning Model shows boxes of equal size, it must be understood that the components are not necessarily equally weighted. Depending on your planning needs for a specific project, you may spend much more time addressing management issues than on message development. Or you may elect to delve deep into market research or be subject to physical limitations in the mechanics of putting your project together. In this model, there are no rules about what items should receive the most or least emphasis. As the planner, you will make the decision, along with your planning team, about what pieces of the puzzle require what levels of attention for your particular project. Nevertheless, it's important not to leave any of the pieces out or you end up with an incomplete picture and consequently, an unsuccessful project.

The model shows the "Media" box resting on top of the other four components. This graphic is meant to convey that media must be determined based on the sound analysis of information from those other components, not that it's the first thing you do or that you should spend the most time or energy there. Media tends to be the fun stuff that everyone wants to jump to first, but building a strong foundation based on the other Ms is critical. It's always more interesting to talk about the vision for a specific exhibit with its exotic bells and whistles than it is to focus on the mission of the organization. Yet without being aware of the mission, how can you be sure that the exhibit in question reflects positively on the organization and helps achieve its goals?

When you work backwards, deciding on your media first and then checking to see whether it can be shoehorned into the mission of the site or the budget or visitor interest or any number of other considerations, chances are good you'll end up spending a lot of money for something that doesn't work very well. Better to back up and think through the other four Ms before getting your heart set on the latest technological gadget that every other visitor center is installing.

Exercises

1. List the four stages of the planning process and give examples of what might be included in each.

2. Contact a local, regional, or state agency for information such as a base map or demographic profiles.

3. Write a Memorandum of Understanding that might help you develop a partnership. Describe how the MOU will be implemented.

4. Using your agency's mission statement (or a personal mission statement if you are not associated with an agency), identify ten activities the agency is (or you are) doing and place them on a mission/money matrix.

5

Management

The management component of the 5-M Model is where those influences of the organization or agency are clearly documented and their impact on the plan is made obvious. The mission, goals, and objectives of the agency or organization should be clearly stated and analyzed to determine how the agency's purpose will be reflected through interpretive efforts. Other factors from the management environment such as enabling legislation, history, policy, issues, programs, and operational resources will be investigated for their potential influence on interpretation. Documentation of previous planning efforts is similarly important and may provide background for important interpretive planning decisions. The interpretive planning process may be used to update previous interpretive plans, but the information and direction of those earlier plans must be addressed, if only to explain why a change of direction is appropriate.

The management section of the interpretive plan is not only essential for the planner but it can be a valuable training tool for interpreters new to your organization or agency. There will be few other places where policy information is pulled together in one place and put in the context of interpretation. For that reason, you may want to consider formatting this information in such a way that it can be pulled out of the interpretive plan or easily reformatted into a handout for staff.

Mission

In reviewing existing documentation, the planner should begin with a search for a clear and concise mission statement that accurately reflects the purpose of the site, organization, or agency. Although the mission statement is the reason for existence, most individuals who work for an organization cannot articulate its mission. Usually that's because the mission is muddied by committee influence, having been cobbled together by people who each needed to get their own pet phrases incorporated. Such mission statements are rarely useful. In fact, the mission of an organization is only as good as its representatives' memories. If it can't be remembered, it can't be spoken. And if it can't be spoken, it can't be applied to daily decision-making. The best mission statements are simple but powerful sentences of a dozen words or fewer.

The mission statement should provide immediate guidance for the interpretive plan by setting some parameters on the site's primary markets and messages. If the mission statement does not provide such guidance or does not otherwise explain the role of interpretation within the agency tradition, perhaps it is time to rethink and update the mission statement.

Updating the mission statement is best accomplished through group interaction and input facilitated by the interpretive planner in a workshop setting. For sites that have a long history and are still working from their original mission statement, it is sometimes helpful to draw on the skills of an accomplished strategic planner for this process, since change of any type can be traumatic for staff used to the "way we've always done things." During the strategic planning session, the facilitator will guide the group through the development of a new mission statement that more accurately reflects the site's evolution over time and its current direction.

Generally, a mission statement should contain no more than three components: 1) some indication of target market (children, families, professionals); 2) some indication of the organization's purpose (inspiring, promoting, encouraging); 3) some indication of service area (the local community, the Pacific Northwest region, the world). Adding information beyond these three elements tends to obscure the intent of the statement and make it hard to remember or repeat.

Because the mission statement should be kept short and simple, gathering group input can be a tricky proposition. Although the input is valuable, it is next to impossible to craft a workable mission statement in a group setting. Instead, the facilitator should gather ideas and key phrases, then work alone to create a simple sentence that sums up the input. The facilitator should then check back with the group to ensure that the revised mission statement accurately reflects the group's thinking. Tweaking may be necessary, but the facilitator should help the group avoid adding unnecessary padding that lessens the effectiveness of the statement. Remember, if it can't be repeated quickly and accurately, it's of little use.

The interpretive plan should support the mission, rather than the other way around. Throughout the planning process, the planning team should

Sample Mission Statements
(specific site identifiers have been removed)

Inspiring leadership and excellence to advance natural and cultural interpretation as a profession.

Reminding people of their relationship to the land through interpretation of the County's agricultural past, present, and future.

Dedicated to the protection, conservation, study, and captive breeding of the giant panda as a component of sustainable economic development of the Valley.

Educating the public about the world's ocean environments.

Sample Vision Statements
(specific site identifiers have been removed)

To be the international voice of interpretation.

To achieve international recognition as a center for botanical research and education.

To have a state-of-the-art interpretive facility known for children's programming.

revisit the mission statement and conduct an interim evaluation to ensure the plan is continuing to contribute to the mission.

The interpretive plan should include the organization's mission statement with a discussion of how that statement will direct or influence the interpretive plan and subsequent interpretive media and programs. This discussion can be short and sweet but it will influence the plan's direction because the mission states why you are doing the things you do.

The mission statements in the sample box all represent good examples, but the best of the examples is probably the last because it says what it needs to in the fewest words.

Vision

If mission answers the question, "What do we do and whom do we do it for?" then vision answers the question "What do we want to be five or ten years from now?" A vision statement differs from the mission in another important way—the mission is designed to help others understand what an agency or organization is all about while the vision is designed to help an agency or organization communicate where it's headed to its own staff and volunteers. Both statements are important to the operation of the organization, and important for staff and volunteers to understand, but mission is more externally oriented and vision is more internally oriented.

Goals

Establishing goals for interpretation is as simple as stating what it is that you expect interpretation to do for your organization. Interpretation should serve a purpose and support the mission of the organization or it becomes the superfluous bit of fluff it is often accused of being. When budget cut time rolls around, interpretation is often the first account code to feel the pain. Although managers who fail to see the value of interpretation in serving the purpose of the organization are taking a fairly short-sighted view, it's not always their fault. Interpreters are frequently guilty of serving their own needs by programming only what interests them personally. The interpretive planner can help bridge the gap between interpretive staff and management by making clear how interpretation can make a difference in management of the site.

Sample Goals (not all associated with the same site)

To maintain the site and historical structures in accordance with the Secretary of Interior's Standards and the county historical landmark designation.

To foster partnerships with other environmental organizations and interpretive specialists in the tri-state area.

To provide education and interpretive opportunities to enhance visitors' understanding and appreciation of the area while protecting and preserving its natural and cultural resources.

To encourage indigenous people enterprises compatible with sustainable wildlife conservation practices.

A case in point can be seen at Yosemite National Park. Bears in Yosemite campgrounds were causing millions of dollars worth of damage each year. For a number of years, eight to ten bears a year would become problems as they confronted campers and would have to be killed when relocation attempts failed. The park invested half a million dollars in a "Bear Aware" campaign that permeates the park. Visitors now watch a three-minute continuous loop video on check-in at the lodges. Cash register receipts

Yosemite National Park's "Bear Aware" program uses a variety of interpretive media to achieve management objectives by influencing visitor behavior.

and parking permits contain "Bear Aware" messages on the reverse side. Interpretive presentations include mention of the "Bear Aware" program. As consciousness has been raised, the number of bear incidents has declined dramatically. Visitors not only understand the problem, but they have come to care about the bears and being part of the solution.

If goals are clearly stated, interpretation can serve a purpose. Goals describe outcomes that will help the organization accomplish its mission. They can be long-term or short-term and they can be very specific or quite general. General and long-term goals are usually associated with a long-range plan or interpretive master plan. A goal may be to gain public support for acquisition of parks or preserving representative ecosystems in your region. Another goal might be to improve the condition of riparian habitat within the sites you manage. Generally, goals are written with words that are not easy to measure, like "enhance understanding," "increase awareness," "encourage participation," or "foster stewardship."

The setting of goals is an important part of the planning process, for goals can provide the overall justification for the interpretive project. If there is no perceived need for interpretation or no sense of what it can accomplish, there is no good reason to move forward with the expenditure of time and money on interpretation.

If there are existing goals for your site, agency, or organization they should be included in the plan. It may be that you will also need to develop goals for the specific planning project on which you're working. In the articulation of goals for interpretation, it helps to ask the question, "What does management hope to accomplish through the provision of interpretive services (regardless of what media is selected)?" When you view goals from this perspective, you can begin to appreciate the wide range of management issues that interpretation can help to address.

Specific project goals for any given interpretive project should align with the mission and any previously stated goals for the overall organization. As the plan evolves, there should be a flow of guidance from mission to goals and on to objectives. If the mission states why you are in business, goals and objectives are those steps that, when achieved, will define success in your business.

Objectives

Objectives provide details about how goals will be accomplished. They are stated in specific and measurable terms describing overall visitor behavior or performance. Measurability is important because it provides the key for evaluating the effectiveness of the plan and its products. Good objectives challenge interpretation to perform, to be more than just fun and games. There have been many discussions about objectives and different resources will vary on how important they are and how they should be written. This book defines three different types of objectives, all of which measure different things, but all of which are important to the success of an interpretive plan. All should be measurable or by definition, they are not objectives.

An interpretive plan will usually include management objectives, interpretive objectives, and action objectives. Each set of objectives will be located in a different place within the plan corresponding to their different purposes. Each objective (regardless of whether it is a management, interpretive, or action objective) should include both the type and the extent of the outcome expected. The type of outcome refers to the specific behavior or activity that is expected, whereas the extent of outcome refers to the time frame, percentage of compliance, or other measurable factor.

Management objectives align with the mission and goals to indicate how interpretation will be used as a management tool. Management objectives will usually appear immediately following the discussion of mission and goals. After the plan's implementation, these objectives can be used to evaluate the success of the project. Management objectives should provide specific time frames as well as other measurable parameters.

Interpretive objectives are associated with a specific program, exhibit, or other interpretive element. Interpretive objectives detail what the individual will do as a result of interacting with the interpretive element. Interpretive objectives usually appear in conjunction with specific media descriptions. (See Chapter 9 for more discussion and examples of interpretive objectives.)

Action objectives define implementation and evaluation steps and should reflect both process and product indicators. Action objectives, sometimes called action items, appear in an action plan or the annual operations or business plan. (See Chapter 10 for more discussion and examples of action objectives.)

Sample Management Objectives
(not all associated with the same site)

Double the number of visitors each year for the next five years.

Within five years, have at least twenty-five of third and fourth graders from area schools using the site for annual field trips.

Recreation-related accidents will decrease by at least ten percent annually.

Funding for other interpretation efforts will increase by ten percent annually through school group payment for education activity packets.

It's important to understand the distinction between the different types of objectives and their application in interpretive planning. Objectives are powerful tools if properly used to suggest guideposts and evaluate success. Perhaps the most important thing to remember about objectives is that they are powerless if not measurable, so suggesting end results that indicate how people might think or feel offers no real benefit. There is no way to measure how people think or feel about something. It's a little like asking, "How much do you love me?" Objectives that measure direct, observable results provide valuable information for future planning and justification for interpretive efforts.

If you have trouble discerning between goals and objectives, remember that goals are generally long-term while objectives tend to be short-term.

LISA BROCHU

Tide pools constructed alongside a universally accessible concrete ramp allow visitors at Yaquina Head Outstanding Natural Area the chance to experience a truly interactive exhibit. Natural tide pools at the site cannot be reached safely without being damaged by visitors.

Goals generally use words like "understand," "appreciate," and "feel," while objectives use words like "describe," "reduce," "increase," and "identify." Objectives are measurable or they are not objectives.

Often, objectives have been used solely to measure output or numbers—how many people go through programs or visit the center each year. While these figures provide good information, they don't tell us much about the effectiveness of interpretation. According to Tom Marcinkowski of Florida Institute of Technology, well-written objectives can and should also measure outcomes and impacts. For example, in the case of the Yosemite "Bear Aware" program, an output might be that 20,000 "Bear Aware" bumper stickers are distributed or that 50,000 visitors will view the video at check-in. An outcome might be that bear encounters in the campgrounds decline by eighty percent annually. An impact might be that fewer bears are being put to death. All of these are reasonable, measurable objectives through which the planner can put a value on interpretation. With thoughtfully written objectives, the assessment of interpretation's value becomes qualitative as well as quantifiable.

This clever sign is large enough to be noticed by humans, but placed where the squirrels can see it. (Okay, maybe it's placed for people who are bending down to feed the rodents, but still ....)

Use building materials that support administrative conservation goals and then take the notion a step further by interpreting their use to visitors.

Policies and Regulations

The interpretive planning process should include a review and summary of all applicable policies and regulations. It's important for the planning team to have a good grasp of the political climate before decisions are made about the site's operations. Knowing the relevant policies help you to avoid operational difficulties and anticipate needed changes. Memoranda of Understanding (MOUs) may exist that will influence partnership opportunities or boundaries of the planning site.

If your project will involve transportation corridors or specific highways, remember to get input from the local authorities on roadways. Planning entry experiences with signs along roadways and acceleration/deceleration (AD) lanes may require approvals from local or regional planning and zoning commissions, so pull representatives from those agencies in at the beginning of the project to be certain you understand the parameters within which you must work.

Key Issues

Every site faces challenges, whether it is a new site in the throes of development or an established site experiencing growing pains. Through discussion with the planning team and through personal observation, the planner must identify the key issues that might affect or be affected by interpretation. Recognizing challenges becomes easier over time and with the completion of several interpretive plans in a variety of settings. Often, site staff are too close to the situation to realize what may be causing some of their problems. In these cases, an outside consulting planner's objectivity can be instrumental in pinpointing problem areas. In some instances, that outside opinion may save thousands or even millions of dollars. For example, one large, well-established nature center near a major metropolitan area felt that its existing building was too small and not user-friendly for visitors or staff. Without going through a planning process, it was decided that a new building was an appropriate solution to the problem. By the time they called for interpretive expertise, architects had already presented a design for an expensive visitor information center that would duplicate many of the functions of the existing building. When confronted with this design, the interpretive planner was able to point out that the new building might create more problems than it solved and in fact, a more economical and effective solution might be to review the circulation patterns of the site and reprogram the use of the spaces within the existing building. Total savings: over $2 million.

The planning process should provide options for addressing key issues. Issues might include staffing or operational challenges, land ownership or management conflicts, demands from user groups, lack of funding, administrative difficulties, old exhibits that must be kept for political reasons, or any number of other significant problems. When the plan is complete, the key issues that have been identified should be revisited to ensure that they have been appropriately addressed through the plan's recommendations.

Operational Resources

Generally, operational resources fall under four headings: staff, facilities, maintenance, and finances. A summary of existing operational resources should be part of the interpretive plan. As the plan develops, the planning team must take the available resources into account and account for shortfalls of resources with staffing and facility plans and budgets.

Inexperienced planners often fail to look beyond the completion of their plan document, leaving site staff with unanticipated problems rather than well-thought-out solutions. Not having operational resources available to accomplish implementation has relegated more than one plan to the dust-collection shelf.

The interpretive plan must either reflect the realities of current staffing levels and capabilities or provide a strategy for acquiring and maintaining the additional staff needed. It does no good to plan intricate, high-maintenance exhibitry if the entire site staff consists of one or two people who must do all things from visitor contact to cleaning. Many sites rely on volunteers for much of their labor force, but the planner should maintain realistic expectations for the use of volunteers in terms of volunteer talents and the time required to perform the various functions recommended by the plan. If volunteers are to be used, their logistical needs must also be planned for within the space program of the facility. The plan should provide staffing requirements with each proposed interpretive element, both for operations and maintenance.

Facilities and landscape features must also be planned or evaluated for the accommodation of interpretive media. A good interpretive planner will assess not only the square footage to be devoted to exhibits, but also any program areas, visitor reception and sales areas, storage, and staff work areas to ensure that they are adequate to support interpretive efforts. For example, if a site has an exhibit shop, it may influence the selection of media, because exhibits can be constructed in-house, but program staff is lacking. Likewise, a planner would want to avoid recommending a personal services program if adequate facilities for preparation and delivery of interpretive presentations are not available.

Maintenance is another operational reality of interpretation. The increasing sophistication of some interpretive media has to some extent been offset with increasing reliability and ease of replacement. However, the basic fact still remains—all nonpersonal media require some degree of inspection and maintenance, which takes staff time and to some degree, specialized expertise, and of course, dollars. The plan should identify existing maintenance resources and capabilities for maintaining interpretive media. Skills that may be needed include carpentry and finishes, aquarium management, live animal care and rehabilitation, electronic repair, computer troubleshooting, landscaping, graphic design, and exhibit fabrication. You can either design around these capabilities (or the lack thereof) or suggest how they will be provided. A typical visitor center with 1,000 to 2,000 square feet of exhibit space will usually need half of a full-time equivalent assigned to interpretive-related maintenance if management chooses to maintain and upgrade its exhibits in a high-quality manner.

Finally, financial realities often color the course of an interpretive plan.

A reclaimed gravel quarry at the Austin Nature Center becomes a recirculating water feature that illustrates a Hill Country sinkhole and creek while supporting a wide variety of plant and animal life.

There are generally two ways to approach planning as it relates to budget. The planner can either start with a given dollar amount and plan within that budget or the planner can put together the best plan possible including strategies for fund-raising to match the recommended capital and operations budgets. Either way, careful consideration must be given to the potential for ongoing financial support of interpretive services and products. As each prescribed interpretive medium is identified, development and operational cost figures should be estimated. The difference between existing dollars and proposed expenditures will have to be raised and operations budgets adjusted to account for the new element.

Revisions and Updates

Like any planning effort, the interpretive plan should be considered a work in progress, even when it is "complete." Things change, as they always do, and the plan should suggest a method for incorporating revisions and updates. In some cases, the suggested method may be as simple as noting in the action plan that an evaluation of all interpretive services be done

Donor signs that are works of art, like that of the High Desert Museum in Bend, Oregon, can attract attention and encourage donations from other visitors.

annually or every few years. Follow-up of that evaluation may include the development of a new plan if necessary. The strategy should include the title of the person or persons responsible for the evaluation and update (staff interpretive specialist, outside consultant, etc.).

Exercises

1. Find five examples of mission statements. Rewrite each example into a simple sentence that is easy to remember, but still adequately communicates the purpose and scope of the organization.

2. Develop a set of goals (no more than five) and management objectives (no more than five) for each of the mission statements in Exercise 1.

3. Visit a museum or nature center and interview the director. What operational resources does the facility have and where do they feel they could use more?

6

Markets

Marketing is frequently a misunderstood concept in the interpretive field. Although it should be a required course for any interpreter because it directly relates to what we do in the public service industry, marketing is often ignored in interpretive curricula because it is considered to be relevant only to profit-oriented corporations. Nothing could be further from the truth.

Marketing is much more than promotions, although the two terms are often incorrectly used interchangeably. Marketing actually refers to the combination of factors that define demand and how an organization will either generate or respond to that demand. Many excellent texts have been written about various aspects of marketing. This book touches on the basics to give readers a simple understanding of the concept and how to apply it in interpretive planning. It is recommended that the reader further investigate books such as Armand Lauffer's *Strategic Marketing for Not-for-Profit Organizations* or *Successful Market Research* by Edward L. Hester for a more thorough treatment.

Every interpretive plan should address the audience or markets it proposes to serve. A market analysis can range from a simple identification of the intended audience to a detailed examination of existing and proposed market segments and the complexities of the market climate.

The important point is that you should understand the market environment in which you are planning to operate and who you intend to serve so that you can determine how to serve them most appropriately. Not understanding your market can lead to tragic misallocations of resources. A major water-recreation area built a visitor center less than a quarter mile from a beach, campground, and boat launch visited by over a half million visitors per year. The visitor center, with a water safety message, only received between 5,000 and 10,000 visitors per year, far below the

The Dallas Zoo's signage targets elementary school children.

average ten percent of annual site visitation that might be expected.

The tragedy was that the recreation area suffered several drownings per year. Had target markets been identified and their desires better understood, the planners might have realized that those beachgoing, boating, and camping market segments had their own objectives in mind, which didn't include stopping in at the visitor center. Most didn't even know it existed. A different approach to the water safety message provided directly on the beach, in the campgrounds, or at boat docks might have been more effective.

Marketing Factors

Make a practice of considering the following elements in the interpretive planning process and your chances of success increase dramatically.

Product. Interpreters rarely think about what they do as a product. In fact, many interpreters have been trained to think that interpretation has nothing to do with the commercialism commonly associated with the term *marketing*. But the planner should be looking at the entire visitor experience as a product, because it requires an expenditure of time and

The San Antonio Botanical Garden took an adventure comic book approach to the signs in its temporary Dinosaurus Tex exhibit targeted to family groups with young children. Observation studies of visitors revealed high interest in the colorful, easily read signs that helped visitors of all ages connect the featured dinosaurs to the plants they ate.

money by the visitor. Demand for the product is based on both the desire and the ability to pay (with time and dollars). Sam Ham suggests in his book *Environmental Interpretation* that interpretation must be pleasurable. His point is well-taken. Because interpretation is voluntary, people must be willing to pay with either time or dollars or both to participate in the experience.

Within the larger product of the experience will be a variety of smaller products that represent specific media elements such as exhibits, gift-shop souvenirs, trails, and programs. Each of these can be packaged as part of the whole by relating the individual piece to a thematic approach that is used throughout the site. (See Chapter 7 for more on developing a thematic approach.)

Publics. There are any number of ways to segment publics into meaningful groups that can be targeted for special attention. Some of the most common segmentation factors include existing and potential; user (external) and support (internal); interest or activity groups and demographics. The decision about how to segment the publics for any given project will depend on what outcome the planner is trying to achieve.

Existing and potential markets is a segmentation tool that can be applied to each of the other categories as an additional layer of information. Who is already coming to the site and who do you want to have come? Existing markets are those who have already been exposed to the programming or mission of an organization. Potential markets might require a different delivery system to reach previously untapped audiences or the development of products that would draw interest from a targeted market segment that may not have ever heard of the organization before. Tapping into nontraditional users allows the agency to broaden its reach instead of only preaching to the choir, but it can be an uncomfortable transition that may require additional training or an attitude adjustment on the part of staff to be successful.

For new sites that have no existing visitors, the need to look at potential visitors is critical. Some of the questions you will need to answer are:

- What audiences do I want to serve?

- Is this the best location to serve those audiences?

- Does a market base of those audiences exist in the area?

- How much time are visitors able to spend?

- What are visitors willing to pay?

- Is there a match between audience interest and what my organization wants to do?

Getting the answers to these questions can be tricky and making assumptions can lead to expensive mistakes. Inviting focus groups, surveying potential audiences by mail or telephone, or looking at comparable facilities may yield important information that is worth the investment you will make in collecting it.

User and support markets are also sometimes called *external and internal markets* respectively. Simply put, user markets are the customers, while internal markets are those who support the program through administration, finances, volunteerism, or other means. It's important to address both internal and external markets, as they rely on each other for success. Some groups or individuals will fall into both categories. The Audubon Society may use the nature center for its meetings, but also provide bird counts and periodically update the bird list. The local historical society may provide docents for demonstration programs and an annual festival, but as individual visitors, they are likely to bring out-of-town guests to the site.

The plan's market analysis should carefully document what your facilities and programs provide for your constituents and what they provide for you. This information gives insight into the markets, but may also have implications for staffing and maintenance scenarios as well.

Interest or activity groups and *demographics* can both be valuable segmentation factors, but it's usually better not to try to mix the two approaches within one project because the complexity of the results thus attained tend to obscure significant and usable information. Interest or activity groups help define what people do on-site, while demographics help define who they are in terms of where they come from, age groups, gender differences, family groups, or ethnicity. Either approach yields valuable information, but it is possible to analyze the audience to the point that you feel the need to customize every experience for each individual audience member, and that's simply not realistic.

Reasonable market segmentation is important to interpretation planning because it helps match the messages to the manner in which they are delivered to targeted groups, increasing the chances that the message will be understood and appreciated. For example, the Austin (Texas) Nature Center's "Babies and Beasties" program is an example of a program designed to foster environmental interaction between parents and toddlers. Such a program must consider the very specific needs of toddlers. (They tend to put everything in their mouths, have limited vocabulary, and may find their own body parts more fascinating than anything you have to say.) As Freeman Tilden suggested in *Interpreting Our Heritage*, interpretation for children should not be a dilution of material presented to adults but follow a fundamentally different approach. Tilden may well have been suggesting that all market segments could benefit from a targeted approach. If he wasn't, perhaps he should have. One agency was extraordinarily proud of the script for its dam tour, which never varied from group to group. When asked what market segments they primarily served, they responded that the local sixth-grade students and field trips from nearby retirement homes made up their two largest visitor groups. The differences between these two user groups should be fairly obvious—physical abilities, areas of interest, age-appropriate references—but because the tour never varied, it probably had limited effectiveness for both audiences. It may take more thought to develop strategies for specific audiences, but if the end result helps accomplish the organization's mission more effectively, it's well worth the effort.

Price

Many agencies, particularly government agencies, are reluctant or prevented from charging a fee for their programs, products, and services. But most interpretive sites will find they are unable to maintain quality services without a good mix of income sources. General admission or parking fees can often be augmented by program fees for optional interpretive experiences. Visitors can self-select the elements of their experience and pay only for those pieces in which they choose to participate. For example, a state history museum charges a parking fee (but has free parking available within a block), admission fee (with separate price structure for members and non-members), IMAX-theater fee (members get two free tickets), experience-theater fee (an ongoing attraction at the museum), special traveling exhibits fee (again, members get two free tickets), and a fee for docent-led tours (members get free tours).

When determining the pricing structure for any interpretive program, product, or service, two factors must be considered. First and foremost, the direct and indirect costs associated with providing the item should be itemized. If costs cannot reasonably be recovered through fees, then another source of funds will have to be found to keep the program functional.

The second consideration must be what the market will bear. Determining this amount will require investigating comparable programs in the area provided by similar providers. Disney can charge $150 for a half-day program because of the perceived value of the experience and because people anticipate spending large amounts while on vacation at a theme park. The local nature center or state park probably can't charge that amount and expect to fill its program even if the length, quality, and program content is comparable.

Some organizations have found that charging a small amount for programs or products creates perceived value. Americans have been trained to expect that you get what you pay for, so they tend to care more for experiences and items for which they pay something, even if it's a small amount. Free, photocopied trail brochures have a tendency to end up littering the trail. The same brochure content printed in full color at bulk prices and sold for fifty cents or a dollar often goes home to provide a lasting reminder of the visit.

Placement

Determining where to locate interpretive features or deliver programs is challenging, but the hotel mogul Conrad Hilton was right. The three most important keys to success are location, location, location. Setting a kiosk even fifteen feet from the right location can result in wasted effort and wasted dollars if visitors ignore it. Knowing the audience and how it typically moves through a site will often reveal the best location for any given media element.

Promotion

It does no good to have the best program or exhibit hall in the world if no one knows it's there or how to find it. Commercial ventures like Sea World often have the benefit of large advertising budgets and a profit-driven motive for success. Not-for-profit groups and government agencies tend to live in the "if we build it, maybe they'll come" mode. Sadly, the latter group may have an important message to deliver that few people ever get to hear, simply because those people who don't normally go to parks or nature centers won't go out of their way to find what could be a meaningful or even life-changing experience.

The interpretive plan should address how the organization can make contact with existing and potential customers through promotional efforts. The visitor experience begins with the decision to visit, so the planner must look beyond what happens on-site to decision points that will influence the customer base. Promotional methods may include media exposure (television, radio, newspapers, magazines), highway signage (directional signs, billboards), publication distribution (flyers, hotel-rack brochures), giveaways (extra tickets, free entries, theme-related products), and other creative methods of getting the word out to targeted markets. The idea is not to blanket the world with promotional materials but to focus efforts on what might reach the targeted markets in the most effective way. If your target audience is inner-city youth, putting flyers up at the park entrance isn't likely to reach that audience. Instead, consider distributing information at places where young people tend to congregate and offer some incentive for attendance.

Getting Market Information

In the initial stages of the interpretive planning process, the planning team should assess existing markets and how they are being served. Staff interviews are one good way of doing this, systematically addressing each interpretive medium and making generalizations about how the medium is used and who is observed interacting with it. Many interpreters carry a small pocket notebook to record observations regarding counts, social characteristics, time of day, and other points of interest surrounding the use of interpretive facilities. This notebook, akin to the field observations of a wildlife biologist, starts to tell the planning team about who uses the site. If systematically collected, informal observations such as these go beyond anecdotal evidence to become a legitimate source of market information.

Head counts have traditionally been used to keep track of those who use interpretive services. Some facilities have electronic counters, either at the entrance facility for walk-in visitors or traffic counters that track the number of vehicles (the number of visitors can then be estimated by multiplying the number of vehicles by two and a half or the average number of visitors per vehicle established for that site). These counts are better than nothing but the real value lies in knowing what those counts represent in terms of social characteristics, learning styles, interests, ability to pay, and timing of use. Head counts can tell you a little about comparative use (for example, seasonal differences) if the figures are collected in a valid and reliable manner.

Guest registers can be mined for revealing comments about existing programs. But bear in mind that the basic premise of leisure activity is that people participate in those activities where they anticipate satisfaction. Most comments will be positive even though site staff may know they could be doing a much better job. For some reason, people often hesitate to offend, even if their honest reaction is less than favorable. How many times have you told a food server that "everything's just fine" then complained about everything from the salad dressing to the table setting as soon as you leave the restaurant? This reluctance to make negative comments carries over to comment cards and surveys as well, so all must be taken with a grain of salt.

If you do receive a negative comment, take heed. Marketing firms follow a general rule of thumb that for every complaint received, at least ten to twelve others have gone unspoken. A sincere negative comment should always be taken seriously. On the other hand, it is impossible to please everyone and occasionally, it's impossible to please anyone. If the site has been forced to close equestrian trails due to hazards caused by heavy rains or begins charging a fee for a program that was once free, complaints are to be expected.

Surveys (in person or by mail) can be a good source of information but the reluctance to be completely honest may color the results. Even the questions themselves can bias the response, so it's a good idea to have an objective third party develop or review your survey instrument to guard against biased questions and response options. For example, if you ask, "Which of the following items do you use most?" and the responses are "A. newsletter, B. magazine, C. workshops," you have eliminated the possibility that the respondent uses none of them or uses them all equally. Avoid putting people in the position of having to answer a question that offers no reasonable option or makes assumptions (like asking someone, "When did you stop beating your dog?").

If you do use surveys, be sure to tabulate the responses on a database where you can cross-reference the answers. That way, you can see if any bias develops due to a specific user group slanting the results a certain way. Check how different user groups answer different questions and you will have even more valuable information that will help you target products to specific market segments.

Good planners learn how to quickly assess existing visitor use through a variety of means. Unobtrusive observation and tracking provide quick insights to visitor movement patterns and interests in the existing setting. Listening to conversations amongst visitors can reveal if visitor interest is sufficiently engaged to remark about the subject to those persons they're with or if there is confusion about the interpretation. It may feel a little like cloak-and-dagger stuff, but getting out and observing visitors reveals reality.

Unobtrusive observation, systematically applied, has many times dispelled myths of management. This tool will often reveal how visitors spend their time, if the time spent is adequate to absorb the interpretation, and if visitors get the full interpretive experience. For example, a state agency installed kiosks in every state park. The kiosks included six large signs heavy on graphic content and few words written in the style of a naturalist notebook journal with the intent of reaching traditionally consumptive wildlife users (hunters, anglers) with a non-consumptive use message (ethics and techniques of wildlife watching). After the first signs were installed in several parks they were unobtrusively evaluated and found to stop a high percentage of visitors but visitors were still not held long enough to read the text before they continued on to their other activities. The decision was made in subsequent plans to edit the text to fewer words and the signs became more effective.

Avoid unobtrusive observation where you and the subject are the only two in the area—it can quickly become obtrusive. You may then find yourself delivering an impromptu survey which defeats the purpose of watching what people do naturally.

A variety of other tools can also be used to assess use. Looking for signs of comparative wear around interpretive features can tell you if interpretation is in the right place for the market segments you want to serve. It can also tell you what experiences people are most interested in having. The pattern of wear at the Wolong Panda Breeding Center in China's Sichuan Province clearly showed a visitor desire to photograph pandas in the natural habitat enclosures. Wear patterns also indicated a significant problem with visitors' lack of respect for barriers between themselves and the pandas, a management problem that can be addressed through interpretation and better landscape planning.

Many organizations are installing point-of-sale information systems that allow sales clerks to enter data with every admission ticket or concession sale. Point-of-sale systems can record general demographic data based on the clerk's observations or actual information such as area code or zip code. This information helps identify where the customer base is coming from, what they look like in terms of age, ethnicity and family grouping, and what purchases are most appealing. The low-tech version of this method is to head out to the parking lot to check the number of rental vehicles, out-of-state license plates, and vehicle types. Though these methods are certainly subjective, all information provides insight and no collection method is perfect. The best of all possible worlds is to gather market information from a variety of sources and put it all into a larger context that is appropriate for the project.

If you don't have the luxury of surveying existing or potential audiences using on-site written or personal interviews, focus groups, mail, or telephone, you can still gather important information through other survey material that may already exist, such as that provided for a Statewide Comprehensive Outdoor Recreation Plan (SCORP), or other regional and local activities. Contact government planning departments or commissions at the local, regional, and state levels to determine what information can best be applied to the project at hand.

Investigating Other Interpretive Attractions

All interpretive facilities occur in some larger context. The market analysis of the interpretive plan will often include a description of that context. For example, several centers interpret the 1981 eruption of Mount St. Helens. These centers might be judged as competing attractions, but to a certain extent, each center is telling a slightly different story with different media for a different market. IMAX, Weyerhauser, and several federal agencies have a presence in the area and all find their niche in this visitor-rich environment. So, in fact, these facilities may be complementary rather than competitive.

Itemizing the other interpretive facilities in the project area is useful to determine what niche needs filling and to identify the potential for partnerships. Visit each facility and note its messages, target markets, and media. Go once on your own and view the facility as a visitor might and then arrange a meeting with the facility's director to determine what opportunities might exist for partnering appropriate activities (staff sharing,

LISA BROCHU

Studying visitor behavior can often reveal important information about the experience desired by the visitor. Picnic tables might be a welcome addition at this roadside stop.

fund-raising, advertising, promotional campaigns, event management). If a facility truly sees itself as a competitor and is unwilling to share information, see what can be done to reframe the relationship into a complementary one. In times of scarce financial resources, sharing is often the best way for each organization to get what it needs.

Travel Patterns and Mode of Travel

Look at how visitors travel within the project region. Do visitors travel from all parts of the city to the facility? Is the facility on regional travel circuits such as from Boston up along the Maine coast or from Los Angeles to Grand Canyon and Yellowstone and back? Is the facility in a day-use, weekend-use, or vacation-destination area? The implications for the type of experience you plan are considerable. How much of an intrusion can you make into visitors' travel plans without disrupting their travels? How are visitors traveling— by personal vehicle, by motor home, by air, and rental car? All can have implications for interpretation. Car travelers may be receptive to well-planned waysides for rest stops and enjoy activity books for children that can travel along after a site visit. Recreational-vehicle travelers increasingly carry

VCR/DVD/TVs and are receptive to sale videos of your sites. Rental-car travelers tend to be more destination-oriented and are good candidates for more extensive and expensive on-site interpretive experiences.

Being attentive to what recreational equipment visitors are carrying or other items they are traveling with can also give valuable clues about your market segments. If the parking lot survey reveals significant numbers of canoes on car tops, canoe-based programming might have a built-in audience. The presence of cameras being carried by most of your visitors could indicate potential success for programs that allow visitors to see the site in unusual ways through the lenses of their cameras. Decals of environmental organizations on many car windows might indicate a fairly well-educated and environmentally sophisticated audience.

Knowing your audience will help bring success to your interpretive plan. Not paying attention to that knowledge will often create visitor frustration. Take the case of a large national park that hosted primarily one-day visits and one-night stays. One night a week, the interpretive staff presented a program exclusively on other parks where they had worked. Visitors there commented with surprising frequency, "I had expected to hear something about this place." At a place where the interpretive staff had one shot with each visitor, they opted for programs that missed the mark, eliminating the possibility of furthering the mission of the organization.

Exercises

1. Spend a weekday morning at an interpretive facility and take notes about the types of visitors who are there and what they're doing. Return to the same site on a weekend afternoon and do the same, then chart your observations.

2. Design a ten-question survey to determine visitor interests at a zoo. Do the same for one other interpretive venue of your choice. In designing the survey, determine the distribution method (entry/exit interviews, cards handed out at admissions desk, etc.) and how the collected information will be used.

3. Read at least two books on marketing principles and theory.

4. Conduct a survey of at least five facilities that appear to serve similar interests in your community. Identify the overlaps and gaps found in audiences, thematic messages, products, services, and administration. Identify opportunities for potential partnerships among the facilities.

Communicating messages is what interpretation is all about. In planning for interpretation, the most appropriate messages can be determined for a particular site based on three things:

1. What are the most significant natural and cultural heritage stories?

2. What are visitors most interested in?

3. What does management need to communicate?

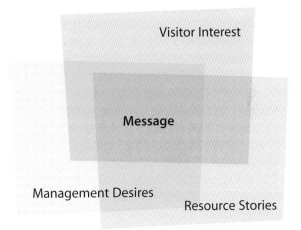

Components of a central theme

The combination of these three components provides the message or messages to be communicated.

Finding the right mix of messages will depend on how much emphasis is placed on any one of these three elements. That emphasis will likely be different for every site, depending on the individual circumstances and the planning approach used. In resource-based planning, management and visitor desires are often left out of the mix. In agency-based planning, the resource and visitor can get the short end of the stick. A danger of market-based planning is to ignore resource

TIM MERRIMAN

The Austin Nature Center incorporates its nature theme into its welcome desk with this colorful tile mosaic.

and management considerations in a misguided attempt to cater solely to visitor interests.

Ideally, the three elements are combined to create a holistic message, but no matter where the emphasis may be placed, care should be taken to ensure that the message chosen for interpretation is appropriate for the site. Notice that one of the key emphasis areas is *not* site staff expertise or interest. This approach is a common mistake that many sites allow because it's simply easier than doing research, making sometimes difficult decisions, and requiring staff to learn new material, but it can have disastrous effects on an interpretive program and the public support the program can generate for the site. For example, let's say you're planning for an archaeological area. The nearest water-based recreation is nearly an entire state away. Evening programs about ocean excursions at this site are inappropriate even if your interpreter is an expert on salt-water fishing and has the slides to prove it. Visitors leave feeling confused and dissatisfied since they most likely came to the program hoping to learn something about the cultures that inhabited the area.

Architectural design elements, like these fish-shaped door handles at the Albuquerque Aquarium, help reinforce the central theme of the site.

Details matter. These lamps at Walt Disney World's Animal Kingdom contribute to the thematic experience.

The key to narrowing down the endless array of potential messages is to do homework, and lots of it. Remember the Information stage discussed in Chapter 4? Gathering information can reveal interesting stories and help you determine what the most significant features of the site truly are. Learn to scan the reams of material that may be available about the site for which you're planning. At this stage, you will not be developing actual text details, but you do need to have a handle on potential concepts for storylines so that you can focus research efforts at a later date. What you're looking for as you scan material are those gems that pop out— the things that make a place special or provide a unique perspective on something commonplace.

In addition to researching written materials, conduct your own site analysis. If you are planning as a consultant, this can be an eye-opening experience. First, ask site staff what they think are the important stories, then form your own opinion. Sometimes, site staff members do not see their own forest for the trees in front of them. Your objective view may point out interesting features and concepts that have been overlooked or taken for granted. As you conduct the site analysis, remember that you are looking for message material rather than predetermining media. In other words, avoid looking at a location and saying to yourself, "I could put a sign there.... I wonder what it should say." Instead, determine your messages and then select an appropriate medium and location to communicate those messages to specific markets. Also avoid falling into the trap of thinking traditionally—that every trail needs signs or every site needs a trail. Sometimes, the traditional media is just not the most appropriate way to go about things.

For particularly large or complex sites, focus groups can help identify potential story material. Hang a large site map on the wall and invite focus group participants to put color-coded Post-it® notes (green for natural-environment stories; blue for built-environment stories, pink for personal-history stories, etc.) on the map to place the stories in what seems to be the most logical locations to tell them. Plot the stories suggested by several focus groups on a single map using a GIS system and you have immediate overlays that show clusters of significant stories. This method can be particularly helpful if the location of a visitor center or trail system is one of the issues to be resolved.

When you feel comfortable that you have identified the potential messages (that intersection between visitor interest, management needs, and significant resources), write a summary of each of those emphasis areas that will be incorporated into your plan document. If there is a compelling reason to include resource inventory lists (wildlife, soil types, etc.), place the lists in your report as an appendix rather than in the body of the document to avoid slowing the reader with details that aren't necessarily relevant to the planning process at this stage. The summary may be separated into three distinct parts, or it can be combined into a single section that may be called a statement of significance or something similar. What you've done is identify the interpretive value of the site—why it's important enough to allocate resources to its interpretation.

Now that you have a plethora of potential messages, you need some way to organize them for planning purposes. There is any number of ways to organize thematic statements, but most processes break down at this point because the planning team can't come to agreement on what constitutes a theme or subtheme or how to group messages in meaningful ways. Consequently, the usual approach is to list every idea that could possibly be interpreted so that no one on the planning team can take offense. Everyone gets to throw their two cents in because surely the visitor must want to know as much as the site staff does about the site. The only problem with this approach is that it does little to focus the message into something that is meaningful to the visitor.

Thorndyke's 1977 research into themes revealed that people have a hard time remembering facts, but they can hang onto themes, particularly if the theme is presented at the beginning of the experience. In other words, they'll get the general idea even if they can't remember the specifics. Yet how often have you seen interpretive centers or attended programs where the focus was on a litany of facts that had no relationship to each other? There is a world of difference between simply listing facts and providing effective interpretation that communicates a message with a specific purpose in mind.

The simplest hierarchy for organizing your thoughts about what stories to tell is the *Theme–Subtheme–Storyline* approach. These divisions are organizational tools to help you through the planning process. Like so much of interpretive planning, the way you approach theme statements depends on a variety of other factors, so there is no one right way to do it. This book suggests a process that works well in any interpretive setting. There truly is no need to lose sleep over crafting a theme statement or developing subthemes and storylines.

Using the analogy of a beaded necklace, the individual storylines can be considered a handful of multi-colored beads. Subthemes are nothing more than groups of beads of all one color (groups of stories that relate to each other). The central theme is the thread that ties all the beads together into a necklace. If you think about it this way, then occasionally you'll find a single bead of a different color, representing a story that may just be better told someplace else because it doesn't relate strongly enough to the main message you want to communicate at a particular site. When you have an odd bead (story), resist the impulse to tell it anyway. Thematic interpretation really works, but only if you let it. Cluttering your communication with stories that don't relate to your central theme ensures that visitors leave the site without a main idea that can provoke further thought or action somewhere down the line.

Some planners find it easiest to begin with a central theme and work down towards individual storylines. Others find it easier to generate a list of potential storylines through a brainstorming session and then organize the gathered information into an outline of theme, subthemes, and storylines. One simple way to do the organization step is to have each potential storyline printed on a Post-it® note. Group similar storylines together and you will likely see the emergence of subtheme groupings. Often, one or more of the suggested storylines will actually work as a subtheme statement, allowing you to group the remaining storylines under that Post-it.® The

Low-tech exhibits, such as this simple bead loom in the High Desert Museum's beadwork collection, can engage visitors in meaningful activity and spark a lifelong interest in the subject matter. Reinforcing the exhibit with appropriate sales items (bead loom, books, supplies) would extend the experience and provide a revenue source for the site.

central theme becomes the common denominator between the subthemes.

Planning by Post-it® is helpful at many points throughout the interpretive planning process because it allows the planner to play with different options in a visual way. It works especially well if working with two or more people so that each can be part of the process by moving items around until all are satisfied.

Avoid the temptation to simply group stories into "natural," "cultural," and "management" topic areas. Although this approach may be appropriate at some sites, it is not usually developed thematically and so results in a conglomeration of topics with a central theme that says something like: "XYZ site is a kaleidoscope of natural and cultural history that is managed for the enjoyment of people." This fill-in-the-blank thematic statement is common, but does not address the real significance of the site or emphasize any particular aspect of the stories to be told. It leaves the visitor to simply figure out on their own if there is anything worth remembering about the experience instead of suggesting something that might provoke further thought or action on their part.

Customized play equipment, like this crawl-through snake at the Portland Zoo in Oregon, can reflect the thematic content of the site and pique the interest and curiosity of young visitors.

Architecture and landscape elements can help visitors connect with the message. The San Antonio Zoo leads visitors into the reptile house with this large tile coral snake.

Central Theme Statement

A central theme statement is the guiding principle for all interpretation at a site (or a given project at that site). It may or may not appear written anywhere other than in the planning documents, but all interpretive efforts should fall within the scope of the stated theme. It defines the approach that you will take with your interpretation. If correctly interpreted through whatever variety of media elements are appropriate, the central theme statement is what visitors will take home in their heads and hearts. When they return from their vacation, and someone asks what the site is all about, visitors should repeat some version of your stated theme (though it's a bit much to expect them to say it word for word, especially if it's a complex sentence).

Much has been written about whether theme statements can be theme statements if they are not complete sentences. The truth of the matter is that a theme statement should work for you as an organizational tool, direct the interpretive approach, and communicate the overall message that you want visitors to understand. If you can accomplish those things with a sentence fragment, or two fragments connected with an implied verb, so be it. It is more important to focus on what you're writing than how you write it. It is often easier for beginning planners to write a sentence than to find a sentence fragment that accurately reflects the intent of the theme and is not simply a topic ("birds" is a topic; "Birds are international travelers" is a theme that provides some direction for the stories you will tell). What you're after is a complete idea that resonates with the audience so that they can remember the concept you're trying to communicate.

Like a mission statement, a central theme statement is almost impossible to craft as a group exercise. Input by the planning team is crucial, but the planner should take that input and fine tune the theme into a simple sentence that reflects visitor interests, management needs, and resource considerations. Once the theme statement is written, it should be reviewed and approved by the planning team before going forward to ensure that it adequately conveys the desired approach. However, avoid the temptation to allow the team to add words for the sake of "clarification." If the general idea is there, leave it alone and move on.

The actual wording of the central theme statement may not appear anywhere other than in the written document, so it is perhaps not the best use of planning time to haggle over wordsmithing that won't matter in the long run. Few visitors are going to come away from the site repeating the central theme statement verbatim. The concept is critical to the success of the overall plan and subsequent implementation—the specific words used are only important in that they convey the concept.

Having said that, you can ease the writing process by generating lists of words that correspond to the three components of management desires, visitor interest, and resource stories. Try different arrangements of one word from each list. If you begin to see a pattern emerge that helps answer the question, "What do I want people to understand when they leave here?" then you have the beginnings of a central theme statement. Work with it until it is easy to understand and interesting. Make sure it connects tangible things to intangible ideas or incorporates universal concepts that will help people make those emotional and intellectual connections so important in the interpretive process.

Sample Central Theme Statements (specific site identifiers have been removed)

What I buy and what I build makes a difference in maintaining a healthy forest.

To protect the panda is to restore the balance between people and nature.

Agriculture sowed the seeds of change in twentieth-century B. County.

This historic trail created connections between people and places in many ways.

Tangibles are those things that can be assimilated through the senses. If you were to ask someone to describe a ring, they might suggest that it's round, gold, has diamonds on it, and is cold to the touch. But if you explain that this ring was given to you by your grandmother and it was given to her by her grandmother and that it was created from the gold that your great-grandfather mined with his bare hands when he came out west, then you might hear descriptions that are more intangible. The tangible thing might suddenly become linked to intangible ideas such as family, adventure, love, work, and inheritance. Now you're making an emotional connection as well as an intellectual one.

There are even some intangibles that David Larsen, trainer for the National Park Service, suggests are likely to connect with everyone regardless of their cultural background. Those "universal concepts" like family, love, and work have meaning no matter what your background might be. Using universals in interpretation helps ensure that the message will be meaningful to every audience member in some way.

In this example of a central theme—Agriculture sowed the seeds of change in twentieth-century B. County—the tangibles are agriculture

LISA BROCHU

A thematic approach to gift shops yields higher returns. Here, Walt Disney World's MGM park invites visitors to spend money on their New York Street attraction.

(farming) and seeds, and the intangibles are change and time (which are also universal concepts). The resource influence is the agricultural setting (the farm that is being interpreted), the audience interest lies with the change during the twentieth century, and the management need is being addressed by confining the interpretation to things relevant to changing land uses in B. County.

It doesn't matter whether visitors leave the site able to state the theme in those exact words as long as they understand that changing agricultural practices were the catalyst for other important changes in the county over a 100-year period.

Subthemes

Subthemes further develop the central theme statement and allow a logical progression into storylines. Subthemes may help guide the arrangement of facilities (for instance, when each subtheme area becomes a "pod" or wing of a building or an area within the site) or they may simply help to organize storylines during the planning process and have no obvious physical

In the "Bug's Life" theater at Walt Disney World's Animal Kingdom, interpretive posters create ambience and provide information about the subject matter.

relationship on the ground. Again, whether they are expressed as complete sentences or not is up to the planner and what works best in a given situation. However, they should be aligned with the theme and reflect some of the same language to ensure that they are in alignment.

Most plans should not have more than three to five subthemes. George Miller's seven plus or minus two research explains that almost everyone can remember five things. Some can remember seven, and few can remember nine. If there are more than five subthemes, the plan becomes fragmented and is probably not doing a good job of relating the central theme statement. The result is that visitors become confused and take away little more than some individual tidbit that appealed to them instead of the overall message the site was trying to convey.

When a smorgasbord of ideas is offered without organization, then what you're telling the visitor is that each idea presented has the same priority. So if, for example, you're creating an exhibit area for a zoo and have proudly listed twenty-five distinct themes in your plan with no central theme, subtheme, or storyline designation to organize or prioritize them, you've

Sample Subthemes
(specific site identifiers have been removed)

Central Theme: *To protect the panda is to restore the balance between people and nature.*

    Subthemes:

a)   *Panda protection begins with an understanding of their specialized diet and habitat.*

b)   *Captive breeding is one step towards saving the panda.*

c)   *Careful husbandry increases the survival rate of young pandas born in captivity.*

d)   *The future of the panda in the wild depends on restoring their natural habitat.*

e)   *The panda has been the symbol of good luck, graciousness, and peace for centuries*

Central Theme: *This historic trail created connections between people and places.*

    Subthemes:

a)   *Cultures came together and sometimes clashed along the trail.*

b)   *The trail cut across the country using landforms and waterways as its connections.*

c)   *The trail became an equalizer as travelers shared many of the same emotions and experiences.*

d)   *You can connect to the trail at a number of locations and in many ways today.*

basically said that the story about camouflage is no less or no more important than the story about conservation of endangered species. Chances are good your mission statement does not require you to tell the camouflage story, but the conservation story may be your whole reason for existence. That doesn't mean you don't tell the camouflage story. You simply find where it fits in the *Theme–Subtheme–Storyline* hierarchy and treat it appropriately so that visitors leave with an understanding of the main idea you want to communicate.

Storylines

Storylines are the details of interpretive content whether they are expressed through exhibits, brochures, programs, trail signs, videotapes, or other media. As the planning and design process continues, each potential storyline will be researched for further development into specific message elements and text components. Storylines can be written in the plan document as complete sentences or as sentence fragments as long as the intent is understood by whomever will be following up to research and write text. Storylines act as road signs for the researcher to help focus efforts and save time in the text-writing and illustration process in the design and fabrication stages for nonpersonal media or to keep program staff on track.

As media descriptions are developed further into the planning process, storylines from the *Theme–Subtheme–Storyline* hierarchy should be assigned to appropriate media. This approach helps ensure that all storylines are being covered in some way. If a storyline shows up in your media descriptions that does not appear in this hierarchy, chances are good that it does not reflect the central theme and should probably not be included in this particular project. (Remember the fishing story earlier in this chapter?) There is a tendency, especially among inexperienced planners, to want to include all possible angles of all possible stories in the interpretive plan. Remember that the planning process is a tool to help you focus your efforts for the most effective interpretation and the plan document should reflect the results of that process. It should not be the repository of the collective knowledge of site staff.

Slogans

Slogans are clever, concise ways to convey a message. The most effective slogans are easily remembered and identified with a particular place or product. In some cases, a slogan may be the same or a more concise version of the theme statement, but it is not necessary or even desirable to develop a slogan for every site. If the site you're planning for can use a slogan (perhaps as a promotional tool), try using humor or alliteration to help make the slogan memorable.

If your site is working with a marketing consultant rather than an interpretive consultant, be sure that the slogan still communicates the central theme of the site. The most effective approach is probably to have the interpretive planner work with the marketing consultant so that everyone involved remains committed to communicating the same message. Otherwise, you may find that the image projected by the marketing consultant is in direct conflict with the messages being conveyed by the interpretive media at a site, making it very easy for visitors to misunderstand or simply forget any message exposure at all.

Exercises

1. Visit three interpretive sites. See if you can determine the central theme statement of each site. If not, ask an interpreter or the director on site if they can explain the message that the site is trying to communicate.

2. Read Sam Ham's discussion of theme development in *Environmental Interpretation*. Adapt the approach to help develop a central theme for an entire site.

3. Read *Personal Interpretation: Connecting Audiences to Heritage Resources* by Lisa Brochu and Tim Merriman. Find the tangibles, intangibles, and universal concepts represented in the themes and subthemes presented in this chapter.

4. In each of the central theme statements presented in this chapter, identify the elements of audience interest, resource consideration, and management need.

5. Develop slogans for the central theme samples presented in this chapter.

The mechanics of interpretive planning fall into two categories—large scale and small scale. These are the physical practicalities, the things that can make or break the interpretive experience for the visitor. Large-scale factors include conceptual thinking about design balance and the complete visitor experience. Small-scale factors include such things as space allocations, site considerations, accessibility, and design-development/fabrication phasing requirements.

8

Mechanics

Design Balance

On the large scale, planners should be looking for what Tom Christensen, Innovations Manager for USDA Forest Service, calls design balance, a blend between site, facilities, and interpretation. In the perfect interpretive site, every visitor who enters the scene comes away treasuring a memory of a pleasurable experience, knowing more, understanding more than they did when he or she arrived. Buildings seem part of the landscape, enhancing rather than detracting from the natural features around them. Thematic elements that reflect the message of the site are woven into architectural design. Personnel look forward to coming to work in settings designed to meet their needs. And best of all, everything is designed to be built and operated within a reasonable budget. This perfect site links inside spaces to outside, creating a zone where visitors, management, and resources come together in harmony through careful consideration of interpretation, facilities, and landscape.

Can such a facility actually exist? The answer is yes, *if* interpretation is considered part of the whole picture right from the start—the common denominator that brings every part of the perfect interpretive site into balance. Most successful sites have practiced design balance to some extent, but many have had to retrofit their facilities to do so.

Berming a building may create the need for negative communication with visitors. Plan ahead to avoid problems by placing pathways where they don't encourage unwanted behavior.

It would be much less expensive and more effective to incorporate interpretive planning at the beginning of the process when building a new site or facility. Architects and landscape architects tend to be receptive to interpretive input if it comes before design decisions have been made. Once those decisions have been made, however, it is often difficult to convince the architect/landscape architect team to make changes. Worse yet, interpretation is often an afterthought, considered only after the site or facility is fully constructed.

Whenever possible, insist upon input into or review of all architectural plans by the interpretive planner before design and construction phases. If the central theme has not been determined by the interpretive planner, how can it possibly be incorporated into architectural elements or be supported by landscape features? Architects have many talents, but determining thematic content of interpretive sites usually is not one of them. In the architectural world, "theme" may have a completely different meaning. The word "theme" is often used to describe a recurring design element (such as a specific color, material, or shape) that may or may not have any relation to

LISA BROCHU

Placement of signs with important messages is critical if they are to be noticed. Here, a live animal exhibit competes for attention and wins against the sign that sums up the central theme and mission of the site.

the interpretive message you want to convey, so be very specific when discussing thematic elements with the architect or landscape architect.

The Texas State Aquarium in Corpus Christi is a good example of design balance. Its entry experience begins with a paved walkway through the Plaza of the Rays where gray pavers embedded amongst pink pavers represent the shadowy outlines of swimming rays. Water features incorporated into the entry walkway allow visitors to cool off in the hot Texas summers by playing in water dripping from the raised flukes of a whale sculpture or the intermittent mist from another whale sculpture's blowhole. Visitors are drawn to the entry doors where they walk through a portal with water cascading past either side, into the air-conditioned queuing area for admission. Inside, the experience continues with exhibits related to the waters of Texas and the creatures that live in them. (See pages 112 and 113 for more on Texas State Aquarium's complete visitor experience.)

The original playscape adjacent to the food concession included a large octopus that allowed children to climb into the dome of its bulbous head and slide down tentacles. (This playscape has since been replaced to provide space for the aquarium's dolphin enclosure.) Exposed concrete pillars have been painted with thematic murals. The exhibit experience comes to a close as visitors are funneled through a gift shop that sells thematic souvenirs ranging from small rubber erasers to fine art.

The entire aquarium experience is balanced—architectural details and landscape features reflect the aquarium's theme of life in Texas rivers, lakes, and coastal waters represented through exhibits, programs, publications, playscapes, and other media. At a site like this, there is no fine line between facilities, landscape, and media. They blend into a quality visitor experience that draws people back time and time again.

Visitor Experience Model

The way visitors experience a site, from the time they make the decision to visit until they leave the site and return home should be part of the planning scenario. Successful interpretation does not exist in a vacuum. It helps shape decision-making at the front end and at the back end of the visit. At each step within the Visitor Experience Model, interpretation will play a role that will influence visitor behavior if thoughtfully planned.

In the **decision phase,** potential visitors will be coming into contact with promotional material or relying on past experiences to inspire them to visit the site. If past experiences were not positive, it is unlikely that any amount of promotions will influence the visitor to repeat the experience. Furthermore, the dissatisfied customer is likely to tell others to avoid the site. But for the purposes of walking a fictional visitor through the experience model, assume that the visitor has either not been to the site or has had a good experience in the past. So the visitor's experience really begins long before he or she gets to the site—it begins with exposure to something or someone that spurs the decision to visit. It is the first opportunity to touch the visitor with the central theme and create expectations for what lies ahead.

The **entry phase** involves more than just the front door. It includes everything that occurs on the way to that front door. On arrival, visitors are looking for clear signals that indicate where to park, how to enter the facility, if tickets are required, what they can do with their pets, and how to address other concerns. During the entry phase, the basic human needs defined by Abraham Maslow in 1954 must be handled. Maslow suggested that people could not attend to personal growth or accept new knowledge until their basic physical needs such as food, water, safety, and security were met. The entry phase provides the opportunity to make people so comfortable with the experience that's about to unfold that their concerns about basic needs virtually disappear. It's also a chance to reinforce the

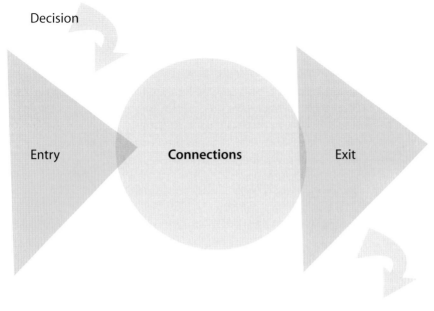

Decision

Entry   **Connections**   Exit

Visitor Experience Model   Commitment

central theme through visual and verbal cues.

The **connections phase** generally takes up the bulk of the visitor's experience on site. This phase includes participation in interpretive programs, viewing exhibits, walking trails, or whatever other activities compose the opportunities available. Ideally, the visitor is exposed to the central theme in a variety of ways during the connections phase, allowing him or her to internalize the message through a complete experience that touches both the intellect and the emotions.

In their 1998 *Harvard Business Review* article, "Welcome to the Experience Economy," Joseph Pine and James Gilmore suggest that today's consumers are looking for complete experiences, characterized by five factors: 1) harmonizing impressions with positive cues; 2) eliminating negative cues; 3) engaging all senses; 4) being thematic; and 5) mixing in memorabilia. Keeping Pine and Gilmore's suggestions in mind while developing the Visitor Experience Model for any given site will help create complete and meaningful experiences for visitors.

The **exit phase** allows visitors to decompress from their on-site

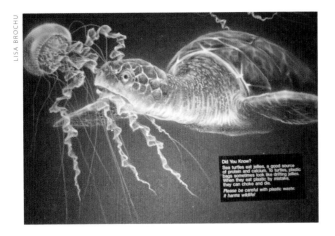

LISA BROCHU

This thought-provoking exhibit is one of the last things that visitors see before entering the gift shop on the way out of the building. The Texas State Aquarium does a good job with selection of thematic souvenir items, but insists that purchases be placed in a plastic bag, that have been seen discarded on the ground right outside the door. Planning for complete experiences means the planner needs to be alert to potential conflicts of message throughout the operation and resolve them for the greatest effectiveness.

Creating a Complete Visitor Experience

The Texas State Aquarium in Corpus Christi, Texas, exhibits many features of a quality, thematic visitor experience.

LISA BROCHU

Wall details imply the motion of ocean waves, while canvas rigging along walkways helps visitors envision a boat on the water. Every feature is carefully crafted to communicate the idea that the Texas State Aquarium is about life on and in the water.

LISA BROCHU

Concrete pillars can be painted to reflect the content of adjacent exhibits like this column of rays at the Texas State Aquarium.

The entry plaza at the Texas State Aquarium incorporates life-size silhouettes of sea creatures (rays, sharks, dolphins, whales, turtles, etc.) with a bronze sculpture and water features to create an outstanding entry experience that sets the stage for the rest of the visit.

Note the shallow pool at the blowhole on the whale sculpture. This whale sculpture periodically "blows," spouting a welcome mist on the hot South Texas visitors.

Inside the Texas State Aquarium, visitor attention is captivated by live hermit crabs and sea stars in the touch pool. The star shape of the pool reinforces the idea of the Lone Star of Texas as well as the more obvious sea star. It also allows more people to participate at one time.

But note what the live exhibit means for the exhibits on the opposite wall. Could the money spent on these exhibits been better used elsewhere?

experience. It's a chance for them to digest the message and consider its meaning. It may include a visit to the gift shop to secure thematic memorabilia before heading to the parking area. If planning a gift shop or food concession, remember to keep the content thematic and the service appropriate. One aquarium had an excellent exhibit about the dangers of sea turtles ingesting plastic bags, yet insisted on packaging all items from their gift shop in plastic bags, many of which promptly became litter on the exit walk or in the parking area where they could easily blow into the adjacent waterway. For the best experiences that encourage further thought or action, be consistent with messages throughout the operations of the site.

The **commitment phase** is what the interpretive program can achieve through good planning and implementation. Tilden's fourth principle of interpretation suggests "the purpose of interpretation is not instruction, but provocation." People should take away a message that helps them make a commitment to positive behavioral change, even if only in small ways. Interpretation can help people become better stewards of their cultural and natural heritage resources if they understand and care about the message being delivered. Effective interpretation serves a purpose and makes a difference. Planners must think beyond what happens in the exhibit hall or a single program and develop experiences that have staying power.

Space Allocations

Ask any owner of an interpretive facility what their space concerns are and most will readily answer "storage." It seems there is never enough storage space planned for those in the interpretive field. That probably means interpreters tend to be pack rats (usually with some very interesting and unusual stuff to store), but knowing that, the interpretive planner can clue the architect to the need for storage space that might exceed the norm. Generally, the following square footage allocations will be adequate for visitor comfort (based on near peak day attendance):

Visitor center lobby: twenty square feet per person
Outdoor plaza: fifty square feet per person
Exhibit gallery: fifty square feet per person
Audio visual area: twelve square feet per person
Interpretive trail: 100 linear feet per person

Be aware that if you plan for peak-day visitation and peak days only occur two or three days a year, the facility must maintain a significantly larger infrastructure than may be necessary. A better approach may be to plan for average days, always with an eye to the possibility of future expansion. Master

Sample Space Allocation for Nature Center

A. Public Areas	Square Footage	Percentage of Total
Foyer	453	3.6
Toilets	560	4.4
Lobby	830	6.5
Sales	575	4.5
Lounge	466	3.7
Exhibit Hall	2,000	15.7
Exhibit Shop	435	3.4
Exhibit Storage	333	2.6
All-Purpose Room	1,755	13.8
Kitchen/Storage	280	2.2
Classroom	575	4.5
Lab	138	1.1
Mud Room	95	0.7
Subtotal	**8,495**	**66.6**
B. Administration		
Director	175	1.4
Development Director	115	0.9
Vol. Coor/Bookkeeper/Sec	218	1.7
Work Room	306	2.4
Staff Toilet/Shower	45	0.4
Subtotal	**859**	**6.7**
C. Education		
Education Director	115	0.9
Three Education Assistants	224	1.8
Volunteer Program Area	487	3.8
Resource Area	588	4.6
Storage	180	1.4
Subtotal	**1,594**	**12.5**
Total Assigned	10,948	85.8
Unassigned	1,807	14.2
Total Building	**12,755**	**100.0**

Placement of signs can make all the difference in their success. Note the small building in the background. Placing these signs at Laurance Lake in Oregon between the parking lot and the restroom almost guarantees that they will be noticed and read by visitors waiting on family members.

planning a new site to be implemented in incremental phases can help sites maintain a reasonable amount of space until expansion becomes necessary, without making the facility appear like it was built by afterthought.

Understanding how visitors behave at interpretive facilities will also help you plan successful interior or exterior spaces:

Panels
- People generally stand eighteen to thirty-six inches from vertically mounted signs.
- People tend to lean on angled or horizontal surfaces.
- Vertical panels have a limited usable space because people can't comfortably read at toe level or above forehead level (keep text between thirty-six and seventy-two inches from the floor).

Trails
- Plan a four-foot minimum width for universal accessibility.

Retrofitting a historic
structure to provide
universal accessibility
can be a challenge. The
unique Dee Wright
Observatory along the
Mackenzie-Santiam
National Scenic Byway
in Oregon solved the
problem by ramping
along the backside of
the structure to avoid
visually impacting the
structure's imposing
façade of lava rock.

- If possible, plan six to eight feet in width with pullouts for groups
  if needed.
- People tend to take shortcuts whenever possible.
- Switchbacks may be a better option than stairs for gaining access uphill
  and downhill if space permits, but use plantings between switchbacks to
  deter visitors from shortcutting.

Flow Patterns
- People tend to turn right if given a choice.
- Older people tend to prefer sequential experiences.
- Younger people tend to prefer scattered experiences.
- Americans tend to prefer a "personal space" that accommodates
  maintaining a distance of about eighteen inches from strangers.

Sequential Experience **Central Experience**

Flow patterns vary depending on management, markets, message and media. Sequential experiences work well if the story makes more sense that way (geologic or historic time lines, for instance); however, there is no guarantee that visitors will follow the sequence or interact fully with each individual element, so there may be holes in the story for certain visitors. Sequential experiences can also be difficult to plan so that they make sense if implementation cannot occur all at once, so this approach may not be the best choice if funding will be available incrementally.

Scattered experiences work well when the story does not rely on a specific sequence to make sense. The real advantage to this approach is that it allows individual elements of the experience to be fabricated as funds are available without significant impact to the overall story. Additions simply enhance the experience but the overall message can still be carried through the individual pieces.

A third option is to focus attention on a central experience that summarizes the theme from which visitors can "bounce" back and forth to related experiences. This option works well when the budget allows for one big splash at the beginning, to be supplemented by additional interpretive elements when later funding permits. The central experience's real advantage is that it offers an opportunity to make the central theme obvious so that it is more likely to be understood by visitors.

Facilities

Estimating square footage needed for interpretive facilities is easier if one has had experience with how people use such sites. If you're hiring an

Scattered Experience

architect to plan and design your interpretive facility, be sure that he or she has had experience with such facilities or have an interpretive planner on hand to help with space programming. The table on page 115 suggests some square-footage estimates for a typical community nature center. Note the allocation for unassigned space—this space will be used for mechanical/circulation space. The architect won't forget to include it, but if you don't plan for it during your initial space programming, you may end up with a smaller exhibit hall, office space, or storage area if that allocation must come out of the total square feet you've requested from the architect.

Capital costs for architectural construction can be estimated using general guidelines in the conceptual planning stages. Architectural construction costs can vary a great deal depending on materials and location, but for ballpark estimating, figure that most facilities can be built for an average of $150 per square foot. So a 10,000-square-foot building would run about $1.5 million, exclusive of landscaping, parking, roadways, trails, and interpretive media.

Facility Reminders
- Specify natural, sustainable materials and building practices that are site-appropriate and help convey the central theme.

- Take into account snow, wind, sun, bug, and water patterns.

- Carefully analyze any potentially hazardous materials situations.

- Be sure that all facilities are as accessible as possible.

- Annual site visitation tends to average about fifteen percent of service area population. If your facility is located near a town of 1,000,000 residents, you might reasonably expect annual visitation of 150,000 unless your site is considered a tourism destination—a place that people plan specifically to visit as opposed to locals dropping in on a regular basis or the occasional casual visitor.

- One to two full-time employees should be employed for every 10,000 visitors, requiring office and storage space accordingly.

- Gift shop operations usually generate an average of a dollar per visitor annually, but could be as high as $1.50 if placed where visitors must pass through the gift shop to exit the facility, especially during special events. Carefully consider placement of the gift shop if revenue from its operation is expected to be a significant income stream.

Site Considerations

Most interpretive planners work with landscape architects (or have those skills) to develop site plans that maximize the interpretive experience. Like architects, landscape architects aren't always familiar with the features of an interpretive site and why planning a site like this is different than planning a grocery store parking lot. In most consumer-oriented planning, convenience is key, but the interpretive experience may require a different approach to help visitors appreciate the essence of the site. Landscape design can be used to slow people down or attract attention to a particular feature.

As you look at the overall site, try to keep roads to the perimeter to avoid bisecting the site and creating circulation problems for vehicles, pedestrians and wildlife. Keep roads and trails away from sensitive historic or archaeological sites and natural features.

Use previously disturbed areas for building and road sites to the greatest extent possible. At the Austin Nature Center in central Texas, the pits left by abandoned gravel quarries seemed a logical site for new buildings, requiring the least amount of disturbance to the natural area adjacent to the site. The pits provided an opportunity to frame the buildings with two ponds connected by a recirculating creek. Within a few years after installation, the creek and ponds maintained healthy populations of fish, birds, and other wildlife and are virtually indistinguishable from a natural water feature.

Complete a hazardous materials review before getting your heart set on a particular location for buildings and site features. Many interpretive facilities have been built on Superfund sites. As long as everyone knows about any potential dangers and the hazards can be mitigated, reclamation of such sites can be an important part of the site's story.

Locate the facility where visitors can see what they are getting into but avoid dominating the site with the main building. The Neal Smith National Wildlife Refuge near Des Moines, Iowa, is an excellent example of siting a visitor center. This graceful building rises from the prairie as though it were just another wave of tall grass. Its low profile suits the site's prairie vistas.

If the parking area is located out of sight of the main building, provide easily seen maps oriented to reality (not necessarily north) so visitors can determine where they need to go. Surprisingly, maps that are not oriented to match the site from the visitor's perspective can be confusing, frustrating, and even dangerous if a visitor cannot easily determine how to navigate trails. Most planners can read maps regardless of orientation, but many visitors cannot.

Avoid having pedestrians cross roads to get to a building. Parking should be immediately adjacent to the building or a trail should be provided to the building from the parking area that will allow people to keep out of roadways. Remember that buses drop off and pick up from the right. A drop-off loop should be provided for universal accessibility to the building, just as all site improvements should be universally accessible to the greatest extent possible.

Design Development and Fabrication Times

Interpretive projects vary greatly in the amount of time it takes to get them done, but the following guidelines provide some idea of what might be required. Using a consultant can move the process along faster if staff time tends to get eaten up with other responsibilities, but due to the nature of contracting, consultants can rarely focus solely on one project at a time. Forty hours of projected work time for a consultant does not equate to one week's work. Forty hours may be expended over two months as the consultant has to work on several projects at once to keep up a steady income stream.

- Letting a contract through agency procurement: two to three months
- Interpretive concept plan: one to three months
- Interpretive master plan: six months to a year
- Interpretive panels planning, design, and fabrication -- 6-9 months
- Publications writing, design and printing: three months
- Audio tape script and production: three months
- Exhibit planning, design & fabrication: one year
- Multi-media planning and production: six months to a year
- Interpretive self-guided trail development: six to nine months
- Visitor center or nature center from initial concept to opening day: two to three years

- Fund-raising: six months to two years
- Reasonable review period for most stages in the process: two to three weeks

Bear in mind that if your site will be under snow or otherwise inaccessible for any length of time during the average year, you need to add that time into your planning horizon. It is generally not productive for a consultant who has one chance to visit the site to do so when there's four feet of snow on the ground or the river's in flood stage.

Guidelines

Guidelines express the standards around which the various media and services will be developed. Guidelines may deal with operations, customer service, visitor experience, or interpretive philosophy, among other things. Generally, guidelines will need to be developed for whatever the project requires, but frequently, the plan will include architectural guidelines, site design guidelines, media design guidelines and operational guidelines at a minimum.

Guidelines may include suggestions about language ("All exhibits and publications will be bilingual."), accessibility ("Moveable parts on exhibits must be capable of being manipulated by a closed fist."), or maintenance ("Trails must be surfaced to avoid the need for daily maintenance."). They may specify hours of operation or the criteria for setting and collecting fees. They may provide guidance for hiring and training of staff or volunteers. Guidelines recommended by the planner help designers, builders, and managers keep the original intent and content of the plan intact, and are especially important if the planner will not be involved in the design, fabrication, or implementation phases of the project.

Exercises

1. Develop a set of guidelines for architectural design of a new visitor center at a state park.

2. Develop recommended guidelines for exhibits at a nature center where the target market is third graders.

3. Visit an interpretive facility and use the following checklist to assess the visitor experience.

Experience	Criteria	Yes	No	Comment
Decision	Are directional signs posted clearly?			
	Are directional signs thematic?			
	Are promotional materials readily available?			
Entry	Is the entry easy to find?			
	Does the entry feature include thematic elements?			
	Does the entry set the tone of the experience or raise visitor expectations?			
	Are positive cues accentuated?			
	Are negative cues eliminated?			
	Are decision points clearly marked and relevant?			
	Is there any indication of ease of accessibility?			
Connection	Can you determine the target market for the site?			
	Do the architectural style and building materials contribute to the message?			
	Do the architectural style and building materials reflect the mission?			
	Are exhibit or interpretive components blended with building components?			
	Are building, grounds, and exhibits well-maintained?			
	Is the floor plan conducive to compatibility of staff and visitors?			
	Does the floor plan help in minimizing conflicts between casual visitors and scheduled groups?			
	Are landscape features relevant to the theme?			
	Do exhibit spaces have adequate lighting and electrical?			
	Do exhibit areas contain adequate storage?			
	Are exhibits easily maintained?			
	Is the space allocation adequate for enjoyment of all exhibits and interpretive components by all visitors?			
	Are exhibit areas and other interpretive areas universally accessible?			
	Does the choice of media help convey the theme and mission of the site?			
	Are decision points easy to understand?			
	Is a thematic relationship evident through on-site visual cues (trash cans, benches, etc.)?			
Exit	Are there reminders of the message on the way out?			
	Would you come back?			
	Would you recommend the experience to others?			
	What would you tell them this place is all about?			
Commitment	Does anything inspire or provoke you to further theme-related thought or action?			

Other comments and observations:

9

Media

Media means many things to many people, but in an interpretive sense, media is anything that helps you communicate your message. Some examples include publications, signs, exhibits, personal presentations, audio or video programs, art pieces, music, guided or self-guided tours, and even landscape or facility design features that support the central theme. In a perfect world, the media palette has unlimited options. In that world, you're free to pick and choose whatever seems to be the best way to get your message across to the markets you're serving. Unfortunately, in the real world, the palette often shrinks in the face of budget, staff, and maintenance/repair capabilities. Given the realities, what are your best options for media selection? You guessed it, the answer is, "It depends."

The complexity of the message, whether the subject or object is actually in view or is more conceptual in nature, whether staffing is available for personal programs, and what type of budget is available all influence the type of media that can be developed. Target markets, maintenance, available space, or any number of other considerations must be part of the decision about what media is most appropriate for a given situation. It would be nice if a dichotomous key could be developed so that media selection would be as easy as following a recipe, but the complexity of developing such a key renders it virtually impossible. There just are no easy answers to interpretive planning.

Because media selection and design are so dependent on the individual situation, this chapter cannot adequately address the enormous number of potential methods to deliver a message. Exhibits, signs, publications, personal programs, and self-guided trails are by far the most common media types, but don't forget about the possibilities of using buildings and landscape, food service and sales items, dramatic productions, music, playscapes, and art as effective ways to communicate stories about the site. When it comes right down to it, media selection is only limited by your imagination and the constraints of budget. Ensure that all media selections are universally accessible to the greatest extent possible. Plan to include a good mix of media types to avoid discriminating against any population group or learning style.

This book is not about design, so there is no discussion of how to develop specific media types. There are many excellent written references for designing exhibits, signs, publications, and other traditional media, but the best reference of all is personal experience. Pay attention whenever and wherever you see people interacting with interpretive media and learn from what you see. Look for ways to improve or adapt what you see at other sites. Take inspiration from things that are not usually considered interpretive media. Children's toys often provide ideas that can be adapted into engaging exhibits, so make a practice of looking at everything as a potential interpretive opportunity and you'll find your interpretive media palette expanding.

Testing Media Choices

Formative evaluation allows the testing of media selections before committing to final design and fabrication. There is no one right way to do formative evaluation. The method selected will depend on the type of media and results desired. The Monterey Bay Aquarium makes inexpensive mock-ups of new exhibits such as their children's play area and gets feedback from visitors prior to designing and fabricating the final version. In some cases, it may be worthwhile to print a temporary sign on adhesive vinyl over masonite (extremely low-cost) to get visitor reaction before investing in a porcelainized enamel product that is long-lasting, but expensive. Today's technology allows more cost-effective formative evaluation than ever before. Although it is often done as part of the design process, formative evaluation should also be a part of the planning process, particularly if the plan includes concept sketches. Simply mounting the sketches and surveying to assess the interest level of visitors can help the planner make adjustments to the plan before handing over media descriptions to the design team.

Summative evaluation takes places after the plan has been implemented. If a contractor is used for the planning process, summative evaluation is often left for agency staff to complete, yet agency staff often do not have time to conduct a meaningful evaluation. If staff are able to conduct the evaluation, results are often not communicated to the planner, especially if the planner is a consultant who is already finished with his or her part of the project. Summative evaluation can be very helpful as a learning tool to refine future plans and to make any possible minor adjustments in media that has already been installed. Ideally, summative evaluation should be based on management and interpretive objectives described in the plan document to determine the effectiveness of the prescribed media.

Writing Media Descriptions

Different plans may require different approaches in writing media descriptions. The following suggestions work well alone or in some combination with each other, depending on the situation and how much documentation of the thought process is needed to help others understand why certain media selections were made.

Narrative Description

Almost every plan will benefit from a clearly written description of media choices. This description helps the reader of the plan understand what the planner is thinking. For the design team, the description provides a verbal image of the piece to be created from which they can produce visual images in a series of concept sketches that lead to construction drawings. The level of detail included in the description will vary depending on whether the planner will be involved in the design stage or whether the designer will be left to his or her own devices to interpret the planner's ideas.

There are no hard and fast rules for what the narrative description should include, but the inclusion of several or all of the following items helps communicate a clear picture to the designer.

Generally, a narrative description should include a **working title** for the interpretive element. This title may or may not become the final header for the exhibit, but it should provide a handle for the planning and design team as they continue to develop design details.

An **interpretive objective** should be developed for the element. This objective may be quite different than the management objectives developed earlier in the process (see Chapter 5); however, the interpretive objective describes a measurable behavior or cognitive function that supports previously stated management objectives and goals. The reason for developing interpretive objectives for each individual element (each brochure, each program, each exhibit) is to ensure that it will actually help to achieve stated goals? Visitors should come away from their interaction with that interpretive element a step closer to the stated goals or it may not be the best use of funds.

Interpretive objectives must be measurable but the measurement suggested must also be reasonable to test. Testing can occur through a

Food items can be considered media elements if they relate to the central theme of the site. The Sweetgrass Grill at Tatanka: Story of the Bison serves up the title character as the main dish.

variety of means, including surveys to determine what messages visitors are retaining, testing devices built into the media (questioning during personal programs or voting devices in exhibits), and observation of visitor behavior.

There is much discussion amongst practitioners and academicians in this field about what constitutes an appropriate interpretive objective. The main point to remember is that objectives are a tool by which success is measured. Keeping the concept of measurement and the definition of interpretation in mind ("a communication process that forges emotional and intellectual connections..."), some objectives should test cognition (intellectual connections). Measuring emotional response is more difficult, but if behavior is an indication of emotional connection (people who care *about* something are likely to care *for* it), some objectives should also reflect observable behavior. Statements that are based solely on emotion or attitude (visitors will appreciate, enjoy, understand, feel, empathize, etc.) are difficult to measure in any meaningful way and should probably be rethought or restated in such a way that results can be tested. It is unlikely that 100 percent compliance can be expected. The individual situation will dictate what

LISA BROCHU

The entry plaza to the "This is the Place" Heritage Park in Salt Lake City incorporates wagon tracks that introduce the story of Brigham Young's journey.

LISA BROCHU

Working with the architect in the planning stages can help avoid problems like glare from windows on graphic panels and exhibits.

seems to be a reasonable measure of success in terms of compliance.

The **location** of nonpersonal media or the venue for personal services should be noted. Ideally, the location will also be keyed to a floor plan or site plan to provide a visual image of the proposed location. The relationship to subthemes or storylines should be established to ensure that the element reflects the thematic guidelines previously established.

A **description** of the item may suggest dimensions, colors, materials, and how the item works. The description should include enough detail that the designer can produce a sketch based on that description. Ideally, the designer would then ask the planner to review the sketch and ensure that the concept for the item has been fully understood.

A preliminary **cost estimate** can be included to help determine a potential design and fabrication budget, but it should be noted that such cost estimates are never considered an actual amount. It is impossible to determine actual cost of fabrication until design development has taken place.

> ## Sample Interpretive Objectives
>
> *At least fifty percent of visitors will remain after the program to pick up litter on the beach.*
>
> *At least eighty percent of visitors will visit two other locations within the park.*
>
> *At least twenty-five percent of visitors will be able to plot the migration route of elk in the region.*

GOS (Goals, Objectives, Strategies) Relationships

This descriptive tool helps show the direct alignment of interpretive media with specific management goals and objectives. It is usually used in combination with a narrative description with strategies keyed to specific items in the narrative descriptions.

Market/Message/Media Matrix

The matrix format allows the planner to ensure that targeted market segments have been addressed with specific media and messages. The matrix can be set up in any number of ways, but generally, market segments go on one axis, storylines go on the other axis, and the resulting intersection boxes get filled in with brief media descriptions or the working titles for media elements. This chart provides a way for the planner to see quickly if there are holes in the plan where messages or markets are being overlooked. It should be noted that not every intersection box will have something in it,

Sample Narrative Description

Working Title: Horsepower on the Hoof

Storyline Relationship: The power that drives the farm has evolved from horses to steam to gas engine.

Text Direction: A short text block will describe how horses were an integral part of daily farm life before steam engines became popular in the 1920s. Another short text block next to the interactive element will describe how the term "horsepower" is used to describe a unit of measure. Next to the measuring stick, a short text block should describe the "hand" measure and encourage visitors to measure the model horse and themselves. Visitors will be directed to try the horsepower under the hood exhibit for comparison to the horsepower on the hoof.

Interpretive Objective: Fifty percent of visitors will be able to identify horses as the original power source on the farm. Eighty percent will view the Horsepower Under the Hood exhibit.

Description: This exhibit consists of a flat upright graphic panel (on the reverse side of Exhibit Element #5) that shows horses pulling a plow or wagon. A strain scale that shows how hard something is being pulled will be mounted to the panel. Visitors will be able to put a strap across their chest and pull against the scale to register how much "weight" they can pull. The scale will compare that force against the force that a draft horse would register. Immediately adjacent to this exhibit will be a full-size model Percheron draft horse with driving harness. Visitors will be able to "drive" the horse using the long reins. If a fiberglass model cannot be found, a lower-cost version could be made of a wooden frame with realistic-looking plywood cutouts on either side of the frame showing the actual size and color the horse. On the panel will be shown a measuring stick with a description of the "hand" measure so that visitors can compare the height of the horse to their own size in hands. An optional audio component of this exhibit will be on a motion sensor that plays quiet horse sounds (munching hay, nickering, tail swishing,blowing, and soft neighing) that might be heard around the barn.

Preliminary Cost Estimate: $15,000

Sample Goal-Objective-Strategy Relationship

Goal: to maintain the site and historical structures in accordance with county historical landmark standards

Management Objectives:

1. increase the size of the oral history collection annually

    Strategy: a. provide oral history recording booth on site (see media description item #11)

2. increase donations from visitors by twenty-five percent to support maintenance

    Strategy: a. provide thematic donation box in prominent location (see media description item #12) **b.** direct mailing to school groups that use barn exhibits (see media description items #1–12)

as some messages may not be targeted to all market segments.

Using the matrix identifies the targeted market for each media element. Targeting a market does not mean that other market segments cannot or will not use and enjoy that element, but a publication designed and written for six-year-olds will obviously employ a different approach than one designed and written for a well-educated adult. Same story, different approach.

Media Costs

Media costs vary tremendously depending on what materials are used and the level of professional involvement required for design and fabrication. Many sites try to save money on media by having volunteers or staff develop text, provide illustrations, or construct exhibits; however, unless these talents are of professional quality, the effectiveness will suffer to such an extent that it may be a false savings. Text writing for interpretive publications, signs, and exhibits is a skill that few people do well. Sites that must save money can do so by drafting text and then having an interpretive text writer polish the material.

Costs for exhibits vary widely depending on design and materials, and may range from $100 per square foot for basic flatwork (no interactive elements, just interpretive panels hung on the wall) to $500 per square foot or more for high-tech interactive exhibits. A good rule of thumb is to

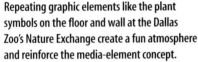

Repeating graphic elements like the plant symbols on the floor and wall at the Dallas Zoo's Nature Exchange create a fun atmosphere and reinforce the media-element concept.

The Austin Nature Center's Dino Pit exhibit features kid-friendly signs that encourage interaction with the outdoor exhibit elements.

budget about $300 per square foot for a good mix of exhibits, unless you've already been given other direction. (Your boss says you have $25,000 for exhibits, period.) So a 1,000-square-foot exhibit space would cost about $300,000 to fill with exhibits. That figure does not include planning and design, but it should give a ballpark amount for budgeting the fabrication of exhibits. To include planning and design, add approximately thirty percent to the fabrication figure. Can it be done for less? Certainly, but when someone asks for an estimate before the plan is completed, these figures tend to be fairly reliable. More accurate numbers can be provided once the plan is complete and even more accurate numbers will be available after the design phase.

Cost estimating is one of those things that depend on the individual or firm doing the estimating. Some firms automatically add a certain percentage of overhead to any estimate, while others add on bits and pieces throughout the process. When asking for or providing cost estimates, be sure to specify exactly what those estimates include and whether they are preliminary "ballpark" figures or a firm bid from a specific source.

Sample Market/Message/Media Matrix

	Grades K-3	Weekend Families	Seniors
Subtheme A: Storyline 1	Outreach program	Trail guide	
Subtheme A: Storyline 2		Visitor Center Exhibit "A"	Souvenir Booklet
Subtheme B: Storyline 1	On-site curriculum		
Subtheme B: Storyline 2	Activity Booklet	Activity Booklet	Visitor Center Exhibit "B"

Average costs (2003)

- Interpretive sign with stanchion: $2,500–$5,000 (includes planning, design, text, illustrations, fabrication)

- Exhibits by square footage: $150 for flatwork, $250 for low-tech interactives, $500 for high-tech interactives (fabrication costs only—add 30% on top of total fabrication costs for planning and design)

- Video programs: $1,000–$5,000 per finished minute

- Touch-screen interactives: $10,000–$50,000 (hardware and software)

- Self-guided trail booklet: $2,000–$5,000 (layout, design, text, and illustrations for print-ready files)

- Simple two-color brochure: $1,500–$2,500 (layout, design, text, and illustrations for print-ready files)

- Short-range am transmitter: $10,000–$15,000 (hardware)

- Trail construction: $10–$25 per linear foot

Exercises

1. Visit a museum, nature center, or visitor center. Analyze several exhibits. Do they relate to the central theme? What is the target market? Are they well-maintained or does it look like it is difficult to maintain? Do they communicate a message to you?

2. For every exhibit you analyzed in Exercise 1, develop an alternative media choice that would do the job better.

3. Attend a Certified Interpretive Guide class (offered by NAI-sanctioned instructors only—see www.interpnet.com).

4. Contact a nature center or museum and ask for its floor plan and site plan. Locate interpretive media and chart visitor flow through the site. If possible, visit the site and see if reality matches your expectations based on the floor/site plan. What recommendations could you make to improve the visitor experience?

A plan may be the best plan ever written, but it is only a dust collector if it is not implemented. To ensure that implementation occurs within a reasonable time frame, every interpretive plan should contain an action plan that identifies the steps necessary for implementation.

The action plan should include specific instructions with suggested deadlines for action steps, including a list of the resources needed to complete the steps. Generally, an interpretive plan will go only as far as describing media, facilities, and site improvements necessary to obtain a quality visitor experience. The action plan, when implemented, will push the interpretive plan to the next stages of design development, fabrication (construction), operation and evaluation.

Design Development

Whether planning personal programs or nonpersonal media, design development fleshes out the plan by providing details of the various media selections. For personal programs, the design development stage is usually called "program development" and includes the gathering of materials needed for presentations, outlining, and rehearsals. Design development for exhibits and other nonpersonal media includes the following items if they have not already been completed as part of the plan development (see glossary for definitions):

- preparation of concept sketches
- research and writing of text
- graphics and illustrations inventory
- layouts of graphics and text panels
- construction drawings (or shop drawings)

The design development stage should provide a fabricator with everything needed to proceed with fabrication of exhibits. In the case of publications, design development should provide

10

What Happens Next

all but the final printed product (print-ready digital files or camera-ready mechanicals). For audiovisual elements, design development might include scripting and storyboards to enable the production crew to proceed with recording, videography, and editing of the final piece. For facilities and site improvements, design development should provide everything a general contractor needs to order building materials and proceed with construction. The idea is that no matter what the end product, the design development stage should provide whatever is needed to complete the process of production.

If the complete project cannot be designed and built in one phase, it is usually a good idea to complete design development for the entire project, then parcel out fabrication as needed to facilitate funding availability. This approach helps ensure that the design will remain consistent throughout the life of the project, which is especially important if the possibility exists that different designers or fabricators might need to work on different phases.

Design development of nonpersonal media is best performed by specialists in exhibit design and fabrication, rather than by site staff unfamiliar with the mechanical requirements of fabrication. What looks good on paper doesn't always work in the real world, and only someone with experience will be able to help you avoid costly mistakes.

Due to the liability and safety regulations involved in designing buildings and landscape features, a registered architect or landscape architect and engineer will often be required to complete design development for buildings and landscape features such as trails, observation platforms, and amphitheaters.

Design development can take as little as thirty days for small projects or as much as six months to a year for larger projects. Be sure to plan adequate time for this important step in your action plan.

Fabrication

This stage is where everything comes together and the ideas expressed in the interpretive plan come to life. For personal media, this stage is equivalent to presentation time. For buildings and landscape features, the term "construction" is most frequently used. Audiovisual programs are in "production" at this point. But when discussing exhibits, fabrication is the phase where the concepts spring into three dimensions. For this book, fabrication is the catch-all term for this stage in the process, regardless of the specific element to be completed.

Fabrication usually requires anywhere from two months for simple projects to a year or more depending on the size and complexity of the project. On the scale of simple to complex, a half-dozen trail panels are simple and a 5,000-square-foot exhibit hall filled with high-tech interactives is complex. Fabrication begins with the design development information and ends with a product installed and ready for visitor use. A number of review steps along the way will ensure that the end result still matches the original vision.

Operations and Maintenance

Just because your sign is in the ground or your exhibit hall is humming with newly plugged-in appliances, don't think the job is over. Whatever is planned must stand the test of time or it is not considered successful. The action plan should address strategies and cost implications of long-term operation and maintenance of visitor services and products. This section of the plan may end up needing more space than is appropriate for listing in action plan steps. If that is the case, it should be included as a separate section of the overall interpretive plan, but referred to in the action plan with specific steps to accomplish the suggested tasks. For example, the action plan would suggest "hire executive director," while the interpretive plan section on operations would include a job description of the executive director and an organizational chart showing how the executive director works with staff and board.

Staffing is only one issue that falls under the heading of operations and maintenance. Though it can be difficult to project actual costs of operation for a given project, particularly if the site is just being developed, the planner can look to similar sites, comparable in size, staffing, visitation, and geographical orientation to get a sense of what the annual operating costs will be. Some plans may require providing a pro forma, a spreadsheet that details operating costs.

Like the staffing section, details of cost estimating should be included as a separate section in the overall interpretive plan; however, the action plan should specify at what point in the process and how funds will be secured to see the process through to its completion.

Evaluation

Action plans should specify when evaluation of the plan or products will be accomplished and by whom. This follow-up step is frequently overlooked in the planning process, since it takes place long after the planning portion of the work is done. Nevertheless, it is important to complete an evaluation of all interpretive services and products, especially those that are newly implemented, at least every three to five years to ensure that they are still appropriate for the site and functioning properly.

ABOVE: The Monterey Bay Aquarium uses a bold and innovative approach to exhibit planning and design reflected in the entry feature of the Crowded Coral Reefs gallery. This exhibit is a kaleidoscope of color and movement that mimics the activity and vibrancy of a coral reef.
BELOW: The Monterey Bay Aquarium plans exhibits that accommodate space for program activities.

ABOVE: **Although the Monterey Bay Aquarium must keep its animal enclosures intact, they keep exhibits fresh for their large number of repeat visitors by changing the thematic approach every three years. This exhibit is part of "Jellies as Art." While one exhibit is on display, the next one is going through a three-year plan, design, test, and build cycle so the aquarium's visitors are rarely exposed to down time.**
RIGHT: **Interpreting the kelp forest of Monterey Bay can be done in any number of ways, including sculpture in the outdoor plaza.**

Before the plan is considered complete (during the planning process) and again after implementation, the recommendations in the plan should be checked for accessibility, sustainable design, achievement of objectives, and ease of maintenance. The series of review steps throughout the process provide an opportunity for ongoing evaluation during the process itself, but an evaluation checklist designed specifically for the project should be included in every plan with instructions on how to use it after implementation takes place. Ideally, the planner should not be the one to carry out the follow-up evaluation, but in some cases, he or she may be the only one who knows enough about interpretation to make an informed report. In these instances, the planner must strive to be objective in the evaluation and willing to make changes as necessary.

Phasing

An interpretive plan may prescribe a long-term project that can take several years to fully implement or it may recommend a short-term project focused on a single product. If everything can't happen at once, the action plan should suggest appropriate phasing to accomplish implementation in logical steps. Factors that affect phasing include:

Availability of staff. Determine whether the implementation be accomplished in-house or by contractors. Sometimes contracting is the most economical and efficient approach even if you have the capability to do the work in-house.

Availability of time. Plan for realistic schedules, especially if implementation will be accomplished by contractors. Few contractors work on only one project at a time, so things may need to take longer than you think they should.

Availability of dollars. In some cases, this factor alone will drive the action plan and possibly the entire interpretive plan. Breaking the plan into reasonable pieces for funding purposes is often a reality that must be considered during the planning process; however, though the plan may need to be implemented in several stages, the final product should appear seamless when all is completed. Good planning and foresight can go a long way toward ensuring that the end result will not appear pieced together.

Priorities for getting the work done through phases must be determined by the planning team. If you haven't already included key decision-makers in your process, now is an appropriate time to do so. Staff, time, and dollars

Sample Action Objectives

PRODUCT/ Process Indicators	Responsibility	To Be Completed Not Later Than
HIRE EDUCATION DIRECTOR	Executive Director	February 2002
Write job description	Executive Director	June 15, 2001
Advertise position	HR Director	September 30, 2001
Conduct interviews	HR/ED	November 30, 2001
Make offer to successful applicant	Executive Director	December 31, 2001

must be balanced against the importance of the story (some site stories may be time-sensitive in their presentation), physical location (some sites are inaccessible or closed at certain times of the year), and tie-ins with special events or holidays.

If your plan involves an opening day linked to a special event or holiday, be sure to leave adequate time for every step of the planning, design, fabrication, and implementation process to unfold at something less than breakneck speed. While you don't want to allow so much time that your process runs the risk of stalling out along the way, you should try to maintain steady progress toward the goal. If, on the other hand, the process becomes rushed for whatever reason (and there are so many potential reasons!), the result will be compromised efforts that are rationalized with an "it was the best we could do given the time" and a large, long, collective, unhappy sigh. Rushing the process tends to cost more in the long run due to the mistakes that creep in and must then be redone at a later date. It's better to delay the opening than to have unsatisfied visitors on the very first day.

One planning strategy that helps ensure that the process clicks off on schedule is the use of process and product indicators which comprise **action objectives** in the action plan. Like every objective, action objectives are measurable. **Product indicators** define the end products. The **process indicators**

Thematic design elements—like this wire fish sculpture seen on a highway overpass along the Columbia River Gorge Scenic Byway—can graphically link sites that might share similar stories.

are the steps that are required to get to the product. Every indicator, whether product or process, should have a specific date by which it will be accomplished (usually expressed as a "not later than" or NLT date), who will get it done and what costs or other resources will be required to get it done.

Other Considerations

Often, issues or concerns will come up during the planning process that are beyond the scope of the immediate project. Avoid letting those issues derail the project, but do include them in the document, as appropriate, under a heading such as "Considerations for the Future" or "Additional Recommendations." Such concerns will probably surface during the information-gathering or analysis stages and may merit mention under a discussion of key issues, but often it helps to repeat specific recommendations as an addendum to the action plan. For example, if the staff or volunteer corps seems sufficient in number, but needs additional training or exposure

At the Bighorn Sheep Interpretive Center in Wyoming, restroom labels reinforce the site's interpretive focus. International symbols prevent embarrassing mistakes by those without a biology background.

Photo opportunities woven into interpretive exhibits provide the "memorabilia" suggested in Pine and Gilmore's Experience Economy Theory.

to professional organizations, making that recommendation in the action plan may generate support for training or membership in professional organizations by management or donors who read the plan document.

Exercises

1. Practice writing action objectives. Decide on a product and list each step that must be undertaken to complete the task at hand.

2. Contact three exhibit design firms and ask for their average times and costs to complete a design/build project for a 1,000-square-foot exhibit gallery.

3. Pick an interpretive site and identify at least three professional organizations or training opportunities that might be appropriate for the staff or volunteers at that site. Visit the websites of those organizations to learn what opportunities they can offer in terms of networking for future planning projects.

Every planning process should result in a product that documents the process. This document should be written concisely, but in such a way that it can be used by the many people who will need access to its information. As you develop your document, think about who will be using it and how.

Agency administrators and boards will use the plan as a management tool, referring to it as justification for upcoming budget requests. For this audience, the mission and goals sections may be the most important in the document. Contractors who will bid on design and fabrication will use it for guidance in preparing their bids and as background material that provides clear direction when they go through the design development and fabrication stages. Media descriptions must be thorough enough to allow potential contractors to pick up the process where it left off, rather than having to start from scratch in the design phase.

Staff will use the plan as a reference tool that comes in handy for training seasonal workers or other new staff since it succinctly encapsulates the significant features and purpose of the site. Fund-raisers may use the plan as illustrative material for funding requests, so the plan must be attractive. Finally, the general public may have access to the plan, necessitating an easily understood, user-friendly format and the avoidance of jargon or sensitive information.

Like the planning process, the format of your documentation will depend on who will be most likely to need access to the information, how much money is budgeted for presentation, and your (or your agency's) style. In any case, the document must read well, be free of grammatical and typographical errors, and capture the essence of the project's importance.

There is no one right way to format a planning document although certain elements are usually

10

Putting It All

Together

Training of staff and docents may need to be mentioned in the plan to gain support of management or donors for this important activity.

common among interpretive plans. If your document is particularly lengthy, an executive summary can be helpful to highlight the key points in the plan and provide an attractive overview for fund-raising or public information. The executive summary should be designed as a separate piece with reference made to where readers can obtain the entire document if so desired.

Inexperienced planners are often tempted to use a template style to format all their documents, following a standard table of contents and using forms to flesh out the document. Although this approach provides a reassuring consistency among reports, the danger of using templates lies in the assumption that all one has to do is fill in the blanks to achieve the desired results. Most people, given the chance, can capitalize on their creativity when released from the bondage of using forms. And of course, very few sites are similar enough that a templated, one-size-fits-all approach will yield satisfactory results.

The following pages include samples of tables of contents. Although the plan documents have some similarities, the individuality of the projects dictated the tables of contents. It should be noted that these are not standard tables of contents, merely possibilities.

Exhibit and Trail Plan

1.0 Introduction

1.1 Purpose of Plan
1.2 Previous Planning Efforts
1.3 Site Description

2.0 Market Analysis

2.1 Complementary/Competitive Functions
2.2 Potential User Markets
2.3 Targeting the Markets

3.0 Summary of Resources Relevant to Interpretation

3.1 Natural and Cultural Resources
3.2 Operational Resources

4.0 Thematic Approach

4.1 Goals
4.2 Central Theme Statement
4.3 Subthemes and Storylines

5.0 Interpretive Media Selection

5.1 Design Guidelines
5.2 Visitor Experience
5.3 Site Plan
5.4 Floor Plan of Visitor Center
5.5 Floor Plan of Self-Guided Tour
5.6 Media Descriptions
5.7 Exhibit Concepts

6.0 Operations Guidelines

6.1 Ownership and Management
6.2 Staffing
6.3 Professional Networking

7.0 Phasing Recommendations and Cost Estimates

Master Plan

1.0 Introduction
  1.1 The Initiative
  1.2 The Center
  1.3 The Planning Process
  1.4 Executive Summary

2.0 Market Analysis
  2.1 Existing and Potential Markets
  2.2 Program/Market Mix
  2.3 Area Attractions
  2.4 Conclusions

3.0 Delivery Concept
  3.1 Mission Statement
  3.2 Goals and Objectives
  3.3 The Hub/Spoke Delivery Concept

4.0 Hub Options
  4.1 Site Selection Criteria
  4.2 Concept A: Existing Museum Complex
  4.3 Concept B: Existing Building near Highway
  4.4 Concept C: New Construction

5.0 Thematic Guidelines
  5.1 Resource Summary
  5.2 Theme
  5.3 Storylines
  5.4 Interpretive Objectives

6.0 Selected Concept Alternative
  6.1 Interpretation Plan
  6.2 Site Plan
  6.3 Facility Plan
  6.4 Operations Plan

7.0 Cost Estimates

8.0 Spokes
  8.1 Suggested Complementary Facilities
  8.2 Potential Partners

9.0 Action Plan

Trail Plan

1.0 **Introduction**
    1.1 Site Description
    1.2 Scope of the Trail Plan
    1.3 The Planning and Design Process
    1.4 Previous Planning Efforts
    1.5 Summary of Current Situation
2.0 **Resources for Interpretation**
3.0 **Market Analysis**
    3.1 Current Visitation
    3.2 Potential Markets
    3.3 Complementary and Competitive Functions
    3.4 Implications for Interpretation
4.0 **The Need for Interpretation**
    4.1 Mission Statement
    4.2 Agency-Wide Conservation Objectives
    4.3 Management Objectives
    4.4 Interpretive Objectives
5.0 **Key Issues**
    5.1 Planning Base
    5.2 Short-Term vs. Long-Term Needs
    5.3 Access
    5.4 Fee Collection
    5.5 Supervision and Maintenance of Site
    5.6 Relationship to Existing Nature Preserve
    5.7 Market Position
6.0 **Thematic Guidelines**
    6.1 Statement of Significance
    6.2 Central Theme Statement
7.0 **Media Concepts**
    7.1 Interpretive Media
    7.2 Short-Term Recommendations (Phase 1)
    7.3 Long-Term Recommendations (Phase 2)
    7.4 Interim Planning
8.0 **Materials and Media Options**
    8.1 Signs
    8.2 Trail Surfaces
    8.3 Suggested Sign Locations and Content
9.0 **Cost Estimates**
10.0 **Action Plan**
Appendix: Memorandum of Understanding

Tips for Formatting the Report

- Be aware of who will use it and how they will use it.

- Write concisely, but creatively to capture interest.

- Number all pages and include a table of contents.

- Use recycled or environmentally friendly products and indicate that you have done so.

- Date each draft and the final product.

- Include acknowledgements of all those who were involved in the process.

- Include photos or illustrations where appropriate.

- Put long lists and detailed information (e.g. wildlife inventories) in an appendix rather than in the body of the document.

- Keep goals and objectives at the front of the document to reinforce their importance.

- Avoid allowing the glamour of the product (the document) to overshadow the process and its findings.

- Clearly state what the plan includes and what it does not to avoid misunderstandings later in the process.

Reviewing the Plan

As you work through the planning process, you will be writing parts of your plan document as you go. Some good checkpoints along the way:

1st Draft Review: to ensure that information gathering has been accurate and complete.

- background information
- resource and market analysis
- mission, goals, objectives
- thematic guidelines (theme, subtheme, storylines)
- options

2nd Draft Review: to assess the further development of selected option(s), revisions to first draft material.

- facility, site, and media guidelines
- media descriptions

- cost estimates
- floor plan
- site plan
- concept sketches
- action plan
- evaluation strategies

Final Draft Review: to ensure that all revisions have been made and are approved

Technical Review: to catch typos only, not to change the scope of the plan

Reviewing the plan document at various stages during the process helps ensure that everyone on the planning team is in agreement with the concept and direction of the project. Signing off on the review documents submitted indicates approval of what has been submitted and direction to move forward to the next steps in the process. If minor changes need to be incorporated, the next submittal should include those changes as well as moving ahead to the next step; however, if major changes need to be incorporated, the submittal should simply be revised and submitted again to achieve approval before moving forward. Specifying a limit in the contract for the number of times changes can be requested will ensure that changes are not requested capriciously without incurring additional expense.

The Final Word

The interpretive plan you create will guide the development of the visitor experience. If thoughtfully approached, it will involve and inspire those who work at an interpretive site with the potential for achieving management goals. Ultimately, the interpretive planner can make a difference in encouraging stewardship of the resource.

Planning can be exciting or frustrating—it truly depends on the planner and the process. This book provides tips to help your interpretive plans reflect the intentions and the effort of your planning team. Applying the 5-M Model will ensure that each of the critical components of management, message, markets, mechanics, and media goes into designing a successful experience that respects the needs of staff, visitors, and the resource. When it's finally complete, what will your plan yield? It all depends—on you.

The following terms may be used differently by different planning and design firms. They are provided here to clarify terminology used in this book and for the benefit of those who may not have had the opportunity to see them defined elsewhere.

approval written agreement that work is accepted as is or with changes as noted. Once approval is given, substantial changes usually require additional services.

additional services work that is not included in the original contract. Additional services must be requested and the cost for those services approved in writing by the client before proceeding.

artifact an original or recreation of an object with historical significance

bid a firm price given to a potential or existing client by a contractor. Services cannot exceed the bid unless requested and approved by client.

bid-ready documents products delivered to the client in such a way that the client can easily duplicate them for distribution to bidders of the next part of the project. To be bid-ready means the client only has to put a cover sheet on it to send it out to bidders with no additional work required.

blackline black and white copy

blueline proofing copy for publications that has all photos, illustrations, and text in place. It looks just like the final publication except the printing is all blue on white paper.

blueprint architectural or landscape-architectural plans printed on a blueprint machine

build fabrication or construction; as in "plan/design/build"

camera-ready layout and materials needed to produce a publication or panel. Camera-ready materials include photos, artwork, and final text prepared in a format that will enable the client to take it to an outputter and receive a final product without additional work or expense (other than output).

central theme statement the central idea that links individual stories together. This can be written as a complete sentence or as a phrase that may also serve as a slogan.

client owner of the project

color comp see *color proof*

color proof a paper print of a publication or panel that enables review and approval of colors as well as layout. Color proofs are one step away from the final product so all artwork, photos, and text should be included in their final positions.

composite a review copy that has all artwork, photos, and text in position. May be black and white or color. Used synonymously with *comprehensive*.

comprehensive a review copy that has all artwork, photos, and text in position. May be black and white or color. Used synonymously with *composite*.

concept plan contents of a concept plan usually include: introduction, description and analysis of site conditions, resource analysis, audience analysis, mission/goals/objectives of agency, theme/subthemes/storylines, narrative description of interpretive media matched to message and audience. May also be called an interpretive plan or exhibit plan, depending on the client's vocabulary.

concept sketch prepared by exhibit designer to convey a visual image of an exhibit description. Details are not expected to be exact as long as the client receives a reasonable facsimile of what the planner has suggested.

conceptual design development of concept sketches and preliminary options for materials

construction documents all specifications, engineering, original artwork, photos/slides, final text, and architectural drawings needed to build a three-dimensional exhibit

construction drawing architectural drawing with details needed to build a three-dimensional exhibit; must be detailed enough that any builder could build from it without additional guidance from designer.

consultant one who provides products or services to clients on a contractual basis, used synonymously with *contractor*

contractor see *consultant*

copyright restricts the use of most printed and recorded material including artwork, sound effects, quotations, etc. Copyright releases must be secured to use any copyrighted material in exhibits or on signs. Be aware that most contracts specify that original material produced for a project becomes the property of the owner (client), so if artists or writers require retention of copyright, this could become a problem if not handled up front.

delivery handing off the product to the client either in person or by mail. Method of delivery should be specified in all correspondence with client.

design providing details regarding materials, sizes, colors, and dimensions. Details can be provided through verbal descriptions, drawings, or three-dimensional models, according to the needs of the project.

design balance when site, facilities, and interpretation evolve together to create a quality, complete visitor experience based on sound planning principles

design details materials, sizes, colors, and dimensions

design development providing design details regarding materials, sizes, colors, and dimensions, as well as graphic layout, original artwork, photos/slides, objects, artifacts, and final text. May include equipment, architectural drawings or engineering required to build three-dimensional exhibits.

design development package the product of design development

digital output final product from a computer printer or plotter, usually used with exhibit panels, signs, or publications

draft text review copy of all words (headers, subheads, captions, instructions, and text blocks) to be used in publication, sign, or exhibit

elevation side view of building or exhibit with no perspective

engineering specific structural details requiring the work of licensed engineers to include in construction drawings. May include lighting plans or other code-relevant items depending on the project.

equipment hardware included in an exhibit, such as audio message repeaters, computers, fans, special lighting, etc.

estimate a general cost figure that may be adjusted as needed when more details are known. Although it should be as close to reality as possible for the client's information, estimates are not binding (as opposed to a bid, which is binding), unless specifically noted as such.

exhibit a three-dimensional interpretive feature. Exhibits usually include a mixture of text, graphics, interactive elements, or objects, and may be inside or outside. The term may also refer to an overall exhibit gallery (the traveling dinosaur exhibit) which then includes individual exhibit elements.

exhibit concept verbal description of an exhibit. Not much design detail is expected at this level, but description should include an objective, storyline, narrative description that explains what the exhibit is about, audience, and cost estimate. May also include a concept sketch to provide a visual image.

exhibit designer the individual who prepares concept sketches, floor plans, and design details based on the planner's descriptions

exhibit detailer the individual who prepares construction drawings based on design-development package

exhibit element a specific exhibit within an exhibit gallery

exhibit gallery a room or rooms that contain many individual exhibit elements

exhibit plan a concept plan that focuses on inside and/or outside exhibits. See *concept plan* and *exhibit concept.*

fabrication actual production of exhibit or sign to the point of being ready to install

final text approved and accepted headers, subheads, captions, instructions, and text blocks for exhibits

floor plan plan view of an entire building or exhibit gallery with locations of exhibit elements indicated. Floor plans may also include visitor-circulation indicators if appropriate

four-color a process or product that uses the four process colors of cyan, magenta, yellow, and black in combinations to create a full spectrum of color

full-color an illustration that uses a full spectrum of color rather (as opposed to black and white)

graphic artist the individual who produces line art or full-color illustrations

graphic design used synonymously with *graphic layout*

graphic designer the individual who prepares graphic layout products

graphic layout determination of the placement and relative sizes of text, photos, artwork, and/or objects. A graphic layout product is a drawing of an exhibit or sign panel, with more detail than a concept sketch, but less detail than a construction drawing. Used synonymously with *layout.*

graphics any artwork, illustrations, photos/slides, maps, or other flat material to be incorporated into an exhibit or sign

graphics/artifact/object/equipment inventory a listing of graphics, artifacts, objects, and equipment that will be required to complete production of an exhibit or sign. Does not include the actual items

header main title

illustrator used synonymously with *graphic artist*

installation putting exhibits or signs into their final resting place by whatever means are necessary to ensure safe and reliable use of the product

interactive something that engages visitors in an experiential manner (as opposed to passive reading or listening). Used synonymously with *interactive element.*

interactive element see *interactive*

interpretive master plan a plan that includes all the elements of a concept plan, but also includes detailed analysis of facilities, landscape (site), and operations issues that relate to or will affect interpretation at the site. Usually includes a site plan prepared by a landscape architect.

layout see *graphic layout*

learning styles kinesthetic (physical movement), tactile, auditory, and visual. Each of these four learning styles should be addressed in a complete visitor experience.

lighting plan architectural details of lighting placement, styles, and wiring required for a single exhibit or exhibit gallery

line art black and white illustration

master plan a comprehensive plan that includes all aspects of a site's operations, including facilities, landscape/site design, and operations

model a three-dimensional representation of an object, usually at a smaller scale than the original. A white model is used to show locations and relative sizes of exhibit elements within an exhibit gallery or within an exhibit to illustrate a building. The white model has few details

mylar plastic sheeting with reproducible copy used to make unlimited copies

object a three-dimensional item

one-color uses one color of ink throughout the product (the color could be black), although various shades (percentage screens) of that color may be used

original that which is produced specifically for a project and from which copies can be made. Contracts may call for all original material to be turned over to the client at the completion of the contract. Be aware of this and substitute "reproducible copy" if possible.

original art artwork produced for a specific project. Always determine and get in writing who owns the copyright for original art produced for any project.

output that which is produced by whatever means, the final product

owner client

panel flat piece that may include text, graphics, or other flat material. Usually used in the context of "text panel" or "text/graphics panel" within an exhibit, though it is sometimes used synonymously with *sign*.

phase an artificial designation of a group of tasks. Use varies widely among clients. In proposals (unless otherwise designated by client), it is used to separate tasks into manageable units to match budget or schedule needs of client (i.e. Phase 1 Planning; Phase 2 Design; Phase 3 Fabrication).

plan documentation of the planning process, also synonymous with *plan view* of site or buildings

plan view an overhead view looking straight down

planning the process of determining the most appropriate media to communicate the most appropriate messages to the most appropriate audiences for a specific site within its operational and physical parameters

primary market the most likely potential or current market segment to be served at a particular site

print-ready layout and materials needed to produce a publication or panel. Print-ready materials include photos, artwork, and final text prepared in a format that will enable the client to take it to an outputter and receive a final product without additional work or expense (other than output). Used synonymously with *camera-ready* (probably more accurate than camera-ready with the advent of digital output) though it usually refers to digital files.

project manager the individual designated as the sole point of contact and coordinator of the project. Should be the only one in contact with client or subcontractors to avoid confusion on part of client or co-workers. Responsible for completing the project on schedule and within budget.

proof to review materials to catch and correct technical errors. Also used synonymously with *color proof.*

proposal materials sent to prospective clients in response to a request for proposals. Usually includes schedule, team, task plan, and budget. Should be used as guide for project management.

publication any printed material, including books, magazines, brochures, maps, bookmarks, etc.

readability index a way to determine the readability of a piece of text. Microsoft Word 6.0 and higher has this feature available under "grammar check" under "tools" on menu bar. Generally speaking, readability should be kept at about an eighth-grade level with seventy-five percent readability.

rendering colored sketch or *plan view*

reproducible copy close enough to original to provide excellent quality on reproduction

research locating maps, photos/slides, and written materials to support text and graphic development

research materials maps, photos/slides, and written materials to support text and graphic development

RFP Request for Proposal. Sent by prospective client to procure potential contractors. Although there are small differences, as a category, RFP's also include requests for quotations, requests for qualifications, invitations to bid, and other similar variations.

schematic used synonymously with *concept sketch*

schematic design design plus text outline and graphics/objects/artifacts/equipment inventory

secondary market a market segment that is likely to be served at a particular site. See *primary market*.

section side view, cross-section showing interior details from selected side

shop drawing architectural details needed to build a three-dimensional exhibit, needs only be detailed enough for in-house fabrication

sign a product that incorporates text and graphics to communicate a message. Can be constructed in a number of ways including fused PVC, fiberglass embedment, porcelain enamel, anodized aluminum, etc. Sometimes used synonymously with *panel*.

sign frame the edging that goes around a sign, not necessarily attached to a mount

sign mount that upon which a sign is placed. May be a wooden kiosk or low-profile angle frame on legs, or some other device. May include the sign frame.

site plan plan view of site showing locations of buildings, interpretive features, landscape features, sidewalks, parking areas, etc. May also show visitor circulation if appropriate

specifications written details regarding materials, colors, finishes, and equipment. A specifications book should accompany construction drawings.

spot color blocks of color on a publication or sign (as opposed to full color illustrations)

stanchion see *sign mount*

storyboard used in development of video, computer, or other AV programs. Storyboards usually include a series of sketches correlated to a written script, from which the cameraman, director, or film editor can determine which shots will be needed to produce the program

storyline basic idea to get across through interpretive media

subhead subtitle associated with specific text blocks

subtheme organizational tool used in the planning process to group common storylines in a physical or conceptual context. Subthemes should directly relate to the central theme statement.

target market the specific market segment for which a media element will be developed

task a specific step in the planning, design, or fabrication process

task plan an outline of tasks used to guide the progress of the project. Almost every proposal will include a task plan that should be used by the project manager to keep the project on schedule and within budget.

text block paragraph or paragraphs of text within an exhibit or on a sign

text outline a guide for developing text, usually provided for each exhibit element, sign, or publication being planned. Should include a working header if appropriate (which may be changed as draft text is developed) and important points that will be presented in the text. A text outline is usually not included in a concept plan, but should be included in a schematic-design package (or in design development when planner and writer are not the same person on a project team).

theme see *central theme statement*

thumbnail sketch used to convey layout of a sign or publication. Usually does not include final artwork or text, though it may include scans of photos and should indicate where text would be located in relation to artwork. Sometimes used synonymously with *concept sketch*.

two-color use of two colors of ink in one product, though various shades (percentage screens) of the two colors may be used (one of the colors may be black)

visitor circulation the way visitors are likely to experience a site, usually indicated by arrows on a floor plan or site plan

wayside an interpretive feature located outside, usually along a trail or traffic pull-off. Wayside exhibits include three-dimensional elements, not to be confused with interpretive signs.

Index